I0428063

BUDGET JUSTIFICATIONS

The United States
Department of the Interior

and Performance Information
Fiscal Year 2015

WILDLAND FIRE
MANAGEMENT

Table of Contents

OVERVIEW OF THE FY 2013 BUDGET

WILDLAND FIRE MANAGEMENT

Overview of the 2015 President's Budget

Total 2015 Budget Request

(Dollars in Thousands)

Budget Authority	2013 Actual	2014 Enacted	2015 Request	Changes from the 2014 (+/-)
Discretionary	784,944	861,482	793,969	-67,513
Mandatory	0	0	0	0
Total Appropriation	**784,944**	**861,482**	**793,969**	**-67,513**
FTE	*3,943*	*3,938*	*4,069*	*+131*
Wildland Fire Management Cap Adjustment	*0*	*0*	240,440	+240,440
TOTAL with CAP ADJUSTMENT	**784,944**	**861,482**	**1,034,409**	**+172,927**

*Note   The 2013 Actual amount reflects the across-the-board rescission (-$1,637), sequestration (-$42,095) and transfers totaling +$10,350 (does not included unobligated balance transfers). The 2014 enacted level reflects an additional appropriation of $28.5 million for repaying NPS, BLM and FWS for funds borrowed in 2013. Those repayments (which will result in a decrease to the WFM account) are not reflected in the 2014 amount in this table. The total FTE amounts shown in this table include 129 reimbursable FTE's in each of the years 2013, 2014, and 2015.

The 2015 Budget proposes to amend the Balanced Budget and Emergency Deficit Control Act of 1985, as amended, to establish a new budget framework for the Wildland Fire Management program that is designed to provide stable funding for fire suppression, while minimizing the adverse impacts of fire transfers on the budgets of other fire and non-fire programs, as well as reduce fire risk, manage landscapes more comprehensively, and increase the resiliency of public lands and the communities that border them. In this proposed new budget framework, a portion of the funding need for suppression response is funded within the discretionary spending limits and a portion is funded in an adjustment to those limits. Specifically, 70 percent of the 10-year suppression average is requested within the discretionary budget caps. The remaining identified suppression need is provided in the requested budget cap adjustment. In addition, our request does not increase overall discretionary spending, as it would reduce the ceiling for the existing disaster relief cap adjustment by an equivalent amount as is provided for wildfire suppression operations.

The 2015 President's discretionary budget request for the Department-wide Wildland Fire Management (WFM) program is $793.9 million. This is a decrease of $67.5 million from the FY 2014 enacted level, which included $28,500,000 for repayments of Section 102 transfers and other uses. As reflected in the table above, a budget cap adjustment of $240.4 million is also requested in 2015. Including the budget cap adjustment, a total of $1,034.4 million would be available for the Wildland Fire Management program, an increase of $172.9 million over the 2014 enacted level.

In FY 2013 and 2014, funding for the ten-year average of inflation-adjusted suppression obligations is split between the FLAME Wildfire Suppression Reserve Fund and this appropriation. The Budget request proposes an adjustment to the discretionary spending limits as a new approach for responsibly budgeting for wildland fire suppression to minimize the risk of fire transfers and provide more stability and certainty of funding to other programs to invest in critical forest and rangeland management needs. The Budget proposes base level funding of 70 percent of the 10-year average of suppression costs to be funded within the discretionary cap. The proposed cap adjustment would fund the remaining identified need for Suppression. The base level of funds ensures that the cap adjustment is only used for the most severe fire activity since it is one percent of the fires that results in 30 percent of the costs. In FY 2015, 70 percent of the 10-year average is $268.6 million. The amount requested in the cap adjustment equals the difference between the total amount of suppression expenditures projected for the fiscal year, based on the Outyear Forecast developed by the U.S. Forest Service's Southern Research Station, and the 70 percent of the 10-year suppression average that is requested within the discretionary budget caps. For 2015, the request for the budget cap adjustment is $240.4 million. The Budget discontinues use of the FLAME Wildfire Suppression Reserve Fund. The DOI and Forest Service wildland fire management programs will continue to strengthen oversight and accountability of suppression spending and use risk management principles to guide decision-making at the strategic, program, and operational levels.

The budget cap adjustment is discussed in detail in the Suppression Operations and the FLAME Wildfire Suppression Reserve sections of this Budget Justification, as well as in the *Budget Process* chapter in the Analytical Perspectives volume of the President's Budget.

The FY 2015 budget funds fire prevention, readiness, wildfire response, landscape resiliency, post-fire rehabilitation, policy, planning, and oversight activities performed by the Department's land management agencies, the Bureau of Indian Affairs, and the Office of Wildland Fire. The program strives to achieve a cost-effective, technically efficient, and scientifically grounded fire management program that safely meets resource management goals. In doing so, every effort is made to efficiently and effectively control the total cost of wildland fire preparedness, wildfire response, and minimize damage or loss to natural and cultural resources in accordance with the Department's strategic goals. The guiding principles and priorities of the WFM are to safely and effectively respond to wildfires, promote fire-adapted communities, and create fire-resilient landscapes through direct program activities and strong Federal, State, and local collaboration.

Other funding changes within the FY 2015 WFM budget include:

- Preparedness – a program increase of $34.1 million, including $15.0 million for tribal resource management;

- Resilient Landscape – program established at $30.0 million;

- Burned Area Rehabilitation (BAR) – a program increase of $2.0 million; and

- Fixed Costs Increases –fixed cost increases of $4.2 million.

The 2015 WFM budget request includes an increase of $25.0 million to strengthen BIA and Tribal wildfire management capabilities and to fulfill the Department's trust responsibilities regarding reserved treaty right lands. This includes a $15.0 million increase in the Preparedness program and a direction of $10.0 million in base funds in the Fuels Management program to conduct treatments that support tribal land restoration priorities on lands where they have reserved treaty rights.

The WFM continues to support the department-wide effort to curb non-essential administrative spending. The WFM bureaus will continue efforts to identify net savings associated with the Real Property Cost Savings and Innovation Plan.

The WFM has developed a 5-year Deferred Maintenance and Capital Improvement Plan. The plan provides the projects of greatest need in priority order with focus first on critical health and safety and critical resource protection. As always, the program has undertaken an intense effort originating in the field to develop these lists.

Specific contributions will be reported through the bureau responses to the savings targets whenever wildland fire program facilities are contributing to savings goals. In 2015 the National Interagency Fire Center (NIFC) will continue to provide office space for fire program employees. Additionally, the Department will continue to implement, in partnership with the USFS, an integrated approach to information technology in wildland fire management, with common strategies, investment decisions, and application management to address business requirements in a cost effective manner.

Government Performance and Results Act

FY 2014-2018 Department of the Interior Strategic Plan

The Department of the Interior FY 2014-2018 Strategic Plan provides the framework for the programs and activities that are performed by 10 bureaus and multiple offices and take place at approximately 2,400 locations throughout the Nation. It facilitates the integration of programs, the allocation and alignment of resources, and collaboration and coordination with stakeholders to achieve key goals. The plan identifies departmental mission areas, goals, strategic objectives, and performance measures. It provides strategic direction for the Department.

The WFM is within Mission Area 1 of the Strategic Plan: "Celebrating and Enhancing America's Great Outdoors." The DOI bureaus implement strategies to mitigate the effects of wildfire and restore burned acres damaged by fire, support communities that are at high risk from wildfire by assisting in the development of wildfire action plans, and effectively use capabilities to respond quickly when fire strikes. The DOI program strives to achieve an effective wildland fire management program that meets resource and safety objectives, while minimizing the cost of suppression and damage to resources.

Ensuring resilient landscapes and fire-adapted communities depends on the implementation of a broad-based, intergovernmental, collaborative, and national cohesive strategy to better address the mounting challenges of escalating fire behavior, increased risk to responders, greater home and property losses, and increased threats to communities.

The Strategic Plan identifies three supporting performance measures to demonstrate and evaluate progress in achieving the national goals to restore and maintain resilient landscapes, promote fire-adapted communities, and respond to wildfires.

2015 Performance Summary

The DOI WFM program has been aligning programs to implement the intergovernmental National Cohesive Wildland Fire Management Strategy, a science-based and innovative, collaborative approach to mitigating wildfire risk. Three supporting performance measures were developed to demonstrate and evaluate progress in achieving the national goals to restore and maintain resilient landscapes, promote fire-adapted communities, and respond to wildfires.

Performance as indicated by most measures has stayed reasonably steady since FY 2010, especially for those measures expressed as a percentage. One notable exception is the "Percent change from the 10-year average in the number of acres burned by unplanned and unwanted wildland fire on Interior land". This measure can change significantly from year to year depending on the actual fire occurrences in any given fiscal year. Actual numbers of acres treated by the Fuels Management program and the various performance measures derived from that fundamental statistic have declined in recent years, as the number of acres treated is a direction function of funding levels.

In addition to the performance measures identified in the Strategic Plan, additional supporting indicators are maintained by the WFM program and are also shown on the following pages.

GOAL PERFORMANCE TABLE

Goal #1: Protect America's Landscapes

Supporting Performance Measures	Type	2010 Actual	2011 Actual	2012 Actual	2013 Actual	2014 Target	2015 Request	Change from 2014 to 2015 Request	Long-Term Target 2018
Strategy #3: Manage wildland fire for landscape resiliency; strengthen the ability of communities to protect against fire, and provide for public and firefighter safety in wildfire response.									
Percent of DOI-managed landscape areas that are in a desired condition as a result of fire management objectives. (SP)	A	35.9% (160,897,47/ 447,806,489)	35.9% (160,788,793/ 447,806,489)	36.1% (161,820,333/ 447,806,489)	35.7% (160,066,449/ 447,806,489)	36.0% (161,212,000/ 447,806,489)	35.9% (160,676,300/ 447,806,489)	-0.1% (-535,700/ 447,806,489)	38.3% (171,310,000/ 447,806,489)
Percent of DOI-managed treatments that reduce risk to communities that have a wildland fire mitigation plan. (SP)	A	80.1% (4,041/ 5,043)	89.8% (2,648/ 2,949)	93.9% (2,736/ 2,914)	75.6% (1,597/ 2,113)	92.4% (1,570/ 1,700)	93.8% (1,900/ 2,025)	1.4% (330/ 325)	96% (2875/ 3000)
Percent of wildfires on DOI-managed landscapes where the initial strategy (ies) fully succeeded during the initial response phase. (SP)	A	97% (6,480/6,655)	97% (7,527/7,770)	97% (9,175/9,454)	98% (6,330/6,482)	97% (7,360/7,580)	97% (7,370/7,600)	0% (0/0)	99% (6,525/6,600)

These new performance measures were established in 2014. For implementation of these measures in 2015, a baseline was extrapolated from historical data.

Other Significant Fire Program Measures

Supporting Performance Measures	Type	2010 Actual	2011 Actual	2012 Actual	2013 Actual	2014 Plan	2015 Request	Change from 2014 Plan to 2015	Long-Term Target 2018
Number of high-priority acres treated in the WUI	A	696,523	705,274	733,871	471,866	495,500	TBD	TBD	530,000
Number of acres in fire regimes 1, 2, or 3 moved to a better condition class (WUI & Non-WUI)	A	WUI 174,347 / Non-WUI 141,606 / Total 315,953	WUI 169,032 / Non-WUI 65,582 / Total 234,614	WUI 231,795 / Non-WUI 102,344 / Total 334,139	WUI 191,780 / Non-WUI 74,139 / Total 265,919	WUI 167,400 / Non-WUI 111,600 / Total 279,000	TBD	TBD	WUI 215,000 / Non-WUI 83,000 / Total 298,000
Number of acres in fire regimes 1,2,3 moved to a better condition class per million dollars of gross investment (WUI& non-WUI)	A	WUI 734 / Non-WUI 568 / Total 1,302	WUI 922 / Non-WUI 358 / Total 1,280	WUI 571 / Non-WUI 179 / Total 750	WUI 1,393 / Non-WUI 583 / Total 1,931	WUI 1154 / Non-WUI 770 / Total 1924	TBD	TBD	TBD
Number of acres in fire regimes 1, 2, or 3 moved to a better condition class-as a percent of total acres treated (WUI & non-WUI) (also a long term measure)	A	WUI 20% / Non-WUI 17% / Total 30%	WUI 17% / Non-WUI 7% / Total 24%	WUI 23% / Non-WUI 10% / Total 33%	WUI 41% / Non-WUI 43% / Total 41%	WUI 20% / Non-WUI 14% / Total 34%	TBD	TBD	TBD
Percentage of all fires not contained in initial attack that exceed a stratified cost index(BUR)	A	18%	9%	9%	9%	10%	10%	0%	TBD

Supporting Performance Measures	Type	2010 Actual	2011 Actual	2012 Actual	2013 Actual	2014 Plan	2015 Request	Change from 2014 Plan to 2015	Long-Term Target 2018
Percent change from the 10-year average in the number of acres burned by unplanned and unwanted wildland fires on Interior lands(BUR) %=difference between yearly acres and 10-yr avg. acres	A	-41% 1,294,546 (-884,429/ 2,178,975)	-38% 1,423,895 (-861,923/ 2,285,818)	37% 3,186,827 (865,740/ 2,321,087)	-36% 1,570,717 (-897,056/ 2,467,773)	0.0% 2,403,600 (3,600/ 2,400,000)	18% 2,402,000 (367,000/ 2,035,000)	18%	0.50% 2,637,182 (12,850/ 2,624,332)
Number of treated acres that are identified in Community Wildfire Protection Plans or other applicable collaboratively developed plans(BUR)	A	594,370	660,673	725,154	368,701	387,000	387,000	0	576,000
Percent of treated acres that are identified in Community Wildfire Protection Plans or other applicable collaboratively developed plans (BUR)	A	85% (594,370/ 696,523)	94% (660,673/ 705,274)	99% (725,154/ 733,871)	83% (389,919/ 471,866)	95% (470,725/495,500)	95% (470,725/ 495,500)	0%	96% (576,000/ 600,000)
Number of acres in WUI treated per million dollars gross investment(BUR)	A	696,523 / $127 M = 5,479	705,274 / $164.98 M = 4,275	733,871 / $132.340 M = 5,545	471,866 / $130.09 M =3,627	495,500 / $87.0M =5,695	TBD	TBD	TBD
Number of treated burned acres that achieve the desired condition(BUR)	A	1,053,945	1,037,658	902,060	4,549,230	1,350,000	1,960,000	610,000	TBD
Percent of treated burned acres that have achieved the desired condition (BUR)	A	95% (1,053,945/ 1,110,844)	97% (1,037,658/ 1,067,892)	88% (1,798,822/ 2,053,270)	87% (4,549,230/ 5,249,050)	90% (1,350,000/ 1,500,000)	89% (1,960,000/ 2,200,000)	-1%	TBD

Supporting Performance Measures	Type	2010 Actual	2011 Actual	2012 Actual	2013 Actual	2014 Plan	2015 Request	Change from 2014 Plan to 2015	Long-Term Target 2018
Percent of DOI and USDA acres in good condition (defined as condition class 1)	F	UNK	UNK	UNK	UNK	TBD	TBD	TBD	TBD

Target Codes: SP = Strategic Plan Measure, BUR = Fire Program Specific Measure, HPG = High Performance Goal, NA = Long-Term Targets Inappropriate to Determine At This Time, UNK = Prior Data Not Available

Type Codes: C=Cumulative Measure, A = Annual Measure, F = Future Measure

COHESIVE STRATEGY AND WILDLAND FIRE PROGRAM MATRIX

Department of the Interior Wildland Fire Management Crosswalk of the Cohesive Strategy Goals to DOI WFM Subactivities and Programs

Cohesive Strategy Goal	Contributing WFM Subactivity	Description of Contributing Programs
		Prevention and Education - Proactive analysis of wildfire causes and the administrative, engineering, and enforcement actions taken to reduce the number of human-caused wildfires. Limiting the number of human-caused fires reduces the overall number of wildfires requiring a response.
	Preparedness	**Fire Management Planning** - Fire Management Plans are created to inventory fuels, fire workload, and management and resource objectives. This analysis and planning process allows fire managers to pre-plan initial and extended attack response to wildfire and provide the most effective and cost efficient response in a timely manner that meets protection and resource management objectives. This process helps fire managers clearly define in advance those areas that require full protection to safeguard values at risk as well as define areas where managing fires for multiple objectives provides the best wildfire response.
		Readiness - The actions taken to ensure a well-equipped and qualified firefighting organization is in place and prepared to respond to wildfires in a timely, effective, and cost efficient manner. Includes the purchase or lease of firefighting equipment, aircraft, and the hiring, training, and qualification of firefighters, fire line supervisors, fire dispatch personnel, logistical support personnel, and fire managers. In addition, this program provides technical staff such as Predictive Services staff that assists in forecasting fire activity changes across the nation based on fuels, weather trends, and burning indices trends.
Respond to Wildfire	Suppression	**Initial and Extended Attack** – Wildfire suppression response emphasizes risk-informed wildfire response that takes aggressive suppression actions when required to protect life, property, and other assets at risk and, minimizes wildfire response actions in areas where risk are reduced and benefits can be derived from managing wildfires to: (1) reduce fuels and future wildfire potential, (2) meet natural and cultural resource management objectives, and/or (3) increase safety by reducing firefighter exposure. Includes the use of government owned equipment and personnel as well as the mobilization of state and county cooperators, contract personnel, national guard organizations, DOD military personnel, and foreign assistance firefighters.

Department of the Interior Wildland Fire Management Crosswalk of the Cohesive Strategy Goals to DOI WFM Subactivities and Programs

Cohesive Strategy Goal	Contributing WFM Subactivity	Description of Contributing Programs
Respond to Wildfire	Suppression	**Fire Severity** - The mobilization and pre-positioning of additional firefighting assets in advance of wildfire activity, due to above normal burning conditions or for burning condition outside the normal fire readiness season. **Emergency Stabilization** - This is post-fire response necessary to prevent threats to life and property damage associated with post-fire erosion, flash floods, and debris flows.
	Fire Facilities	**Deferred Maintenance and Construction** - This program provides the necessary facilities to house firefighters and provide operational centers for wildfire response crews in close proximity to those areas where wildfire activity occurs. This allows timely response to reduce the potential of fires becoming large and expensive.
	Fuels Management	**Fuels Treatments** – Fuels treatments and activities are designed to improve the integrity and resilience of our forests and rangelands; contribute to community adaptation to fire; and/or improve the ability to safely and appropriately respond to wildfire. Fuels treatments contribute to wildfire response by reducing fuels to change fire behavior characteristics, which may increase wildfire management options.
Fire Adapted Communities	Fuels Management	**Mitigation and Education** - Educates homeowners and communities about practices that make their homes more fire resistant and fire safe. Promotes a shared responsibility through the creation of defensible space around homes from which firefighters can safely fight wildfires. **Community Wildfire Protection Plans** - Provides assistance to communities to develop Community Wildfire Protection Plans that make their communities more resistant to and defensible against wildfires. These plans identify treatment actions to reduce wildfire threats and plan important information such as wildfire evacuation routes in advance of wildfires occurring. **Fuels Treatments-** Provides for specific treatment of fuels adjacent to and within communities to reduce wildfire ignitions, spread, and fire intensity.

Department of the Interior Wildland Fire Management Crosswalk of the Cohesive Strategy Goals to DOI WFM Sub activities and Programs

Cohesive Strategy Goal	Contributing WFM Subactivity	Description of Contributing Programs
Fire Adapted Communities	Joint Fire Science Program (JFSP)	**Joint Fire Science Program** - Focuses on questions of high priority to fire and fuels managers by conducting roundtables to identify critical issues, and developing science plans to guide integrated research leading to significant deliverables. Research conducted by JFSP has contributed to knowledge in managing fire, fuels and community assistance.
Restore and Maintain Resilient Landscapes	Resilient Landscapes	**Landscape Restoration** - These treatments are used to restore ecological health and vigor to areas that have seen an ecological decline due to altered fire regimes, other ecological disturbances, or environmental impacts that have disrupted the ecosystem health. These treatments may change species composition, stocking, levels, and reduce the presence of invasive, non-native species. Restoration activities of these areas often make them more resilient to the impacts of wildfires in the future.
	Burned Area Rehabilitation	**Post-fire Rehabilitation** - Post-fire rehabilitation activities strive to rehabilitate areas damaged by fire by stabilizing ecosystems and providing the proper conditions for natural re-vegetation and/or providing the necessary re-vegetation resources so that an ecosystem can progress toward recovery before noxious weeds and introduced species become established. Often introduced species are more flammable and may contribute to future wildfire spread and severity. By creating an environment favorable to rehabilitation this program enhances ecosystem health and makes areas more resilient to future wildfires.

Department of the Interior Wildland Fire Management Crosswalk of the Cohesive Strategy Goals to DOI WFM Sub activities and Programs

Cohesive Strategy Goal	Contributing WFM Subactivity	Description of Contributing Programs
Restore and Maintain Resilient Landscapes	Fuels Management	**Mitigation and Education** – Provides funding and assistance to communities to mitigate the threat and impact of wildfire. Educates homeowners and communities about practices that make their homes more fire resistant and fire safe. Promotes creation of defensible space around homes from which firefighters can safely fight wildfires.
		Community Wildfire Protection Plans - Provides assistance to communities to develop Community Wildfire Protection Plans that make their communities more resistant to and defensible against wildfires. These plans identify treatment actions to reduce wildfire threats and plan important information such as wildfire evacuation routes and emergency shelter locations when a fire occurs.
		Fuels Treatments- Fuels treatments and activities are designed to improve the integrity and resilience of our forests and rangelands, including the WUI; contribute to community adaptation to fire; and/or improve the ability to safely and appropriately respond to wildfire. Fuels treatments adjacent to and within communities are implemented to reduce wildfire spread, fire intensity and damage to communities and their values.

BUDGET TABLES

Department-Wide Wildland Fire Management 2015 Budgetary Changes at a Glance (Dollars in Thousands)					
Appropriation: Wildland Fire Management 14X1125	2013 Actual	2014 Enacted	Fixed Costs	Program Changes	2015 President's Budget
Preparedness	264,833	281,928	+2,947	+34,095	318,970
Fixed Costs			[2,947]		
Program Increase – BIA Tribal Contract & Admin Support				[9,000]	
Program Increase – BIA Workforce Development				[6,000]	
Program Increase – Maintain Veterans Crews				[1,700]	
Program Increase – Firefighter and Support Personnel				[5,395]	
Program Increase – Aviation Program Contracts				[10,000]	
Program Increase – Equipment Capitalization				[2,000]	
Suppression Operations	261,206	285,878	-	-17,318	268,560
Program Decrease 2015 – 70% of 10 Year Suppression Average Adjustment				[-17,318]	
FLAME Transfer	91,669				
Sequestration of FLAME transfer	-4,621				
Other Operations					
Hazardous Fuels Reduction	137,685	145,024	+1,263	-	146,287
Fixed Costs			[1,263]		
Resilient Landscape	-	-	-	+30,000	30,000
Establish Activity - 2015			-	[+30,000]	
Burned Area Rehabilitation	12,341	16,035	-	+2,000	18,035
Program Increase - 2015				[+2,000]	
Fire Facilities	5,806	6,127	-	-	6,127
Joint Fire Science	5,675	5,990	-	-	5,990
TOTAL, WILDLAND FIRE APPROPRIATION (Without Section 102 Transfers)	774,594	740,982	+4,210	+ 48,777	793,969

Department-Wide Wildland Fire Management
2015 Budgetary Changes at a Glance
(Dollars in Thousands)

Appropriation: Wildland Fire Management 14X1125	2013 Actual	2014 Enacted	Fixed Costs	Program Changes	2015 President's Budget
Appropriation-Borrowing Repayment	15,500	28,500	-	-28,500	-
Transfer – Repayment of Section 102	-15,500	-	-	-	-
2013 Sec 102 Transfers for Suppression	6,136	-	-	-	-
Net Other Transfers	4,214	-	-	-	-
TOTAL, WILDLAND FIRE APPROPRIATION (With Rescissions and Transfers)	784,944	769,482	+4,210	+20,277	793,969

Appropriation: FLAME Wildfire Suppression Reserve Fund 14X1127	2013 Actual	2014 Enacted	Fixed Costs	Program Changes	2015 President's Budget
Suppression Operations	91,669	92,000	-	-92,000	-
FLAME Transfer to Suppression Operations	-91,669				
Program Decrease				[-92,000]	
TOTAL, FLAME WILDFIRE SUPPRESSION RESERVE FUND	-	92,000	-	-92,000	-

	2013 Actual	2014 Enacted	Fixed Costs	Program Changes	2015 President's Budget
TOTAL, ALL DEPARTMENT WIDE WILDLAND FIRE MANAGEMENT (without Cap Adjustment)	784,944	861,482	+4,210	-71,723	793,969
Wildland Fire Management Cap Adjustment					240,440
TOTAL WILDLAND FIRE MANAGEMENT WITH CAP ADJUSTMENT					1,034,409

Summary of Requirements for Wildland Fire Management Program
(Dollars in Thousands)

	2013 Amount	2014 Total FTE	2014 Amount	Fixed Costs & Related Transfers (+/-)	Internal Transfers (+/-)	Program Changes FTE (+/-)	Program Changes Amount (+/-)	2015 FTE	2015 Amount	Change from CY FTE (+/-)	Change from CY Amount (+/-)
Wildland Fire Management											
Preparedness	264,833	2,277	281,928	+2,947	+131	-	+34,095	2,408	318,970	+131	37,042
Suppression Operations	261,206	470	285,878	(17,318)	+0	+0	-	470	268,560	+0	(17,318)
FLAME Transfer	91,669	-	-	+0	+0	+0	-	-	-	-	-
Sequester FLAME Transfer	(4,621)	-	-	-	-	-	-	-	-	-	-
Other Operations											
Fuels Management	137,685	1,013	145,024	+1,263	+0	-	-	1,013	146,287	+0	1,263
Resilient Landscapes	-	-	-	+0	+0	+0	+30,000	0	30,000	+0	30,000
Burned Area Rehabilitation	12,341	45	16,035	+0	+0	+0	+2,000	45	18,035	+0	2,000
Fire Facilities	5,806	0	6,127	+0	+0	+0	-	0	6,127	+0	-
Joint Fire Science	5,675	4	5,990	+0	+0	+0	-	4	5,990	+0	-
Total Other Operations	161,507	1,062	173,176	+1,263	+0	+0	+32,000	1,062	206,439	+0	33,263
Subtotal, without Transfers	774,594	3,809	740,982	+4,210	+0	+131	48,777	3,940	793,969	+131	52,987
Appropriation - Borrowing Repayment	15,500		28,500	-	-	-	(28,500)	0	-	+0	(28,500)
Transfer - Repayment of Section 102	(15,500)	-	-	-	-	-	-	0	-	+0	-
2013 Section 102 Transfers for Suppression	6,136	-	-	-	-	-	-	0	-	+0	-
Net Other Transfers	4,214	-	-	-	-	-	-	0	-	+0	-
Total Wildland Fire Appropriation	784,944	3,809	769,482	+4,210	-	+131	20,277	3,940	793,969	+131	24,487
FLAME Wildland Fire Suppression Operations	91,669	-	92,000	+0	-	+0	(92,000)	-	-	+0	(92,000)
Transfer to Suppression Operations	(91,669)	-	-	+0	-	+0	240,440	0	240,440	+0	240,440
Total All Department Wide Wildland Fire Management (without Cap Adjustment)	784,944	3,809	769,482	+4,210	-	+131	20,277	3,940	793,969	+131	24,487
Wildland Fire Management Cap Adjustment	-	-	-	-	-	-	240,440	-	240,440	-	240,440
Total Wildland Fire with Cap Adjustment	784,944	3,809	769,482	+4,210	-	+131	260,717	3,940	1,034,409	+131	264,927

Wildland Fire Management
Justification of Fixed Costs and Internal Realignments
(Dollars In Thousands)

Fixed Cost Changes and Projections	2014 Total or Change	2014 to 2015 Change
Change in Number of Paid Days		
This column reflects changes in pay associated with the change in the number of paid days between the CY and BY. In years where there is no change in paid days, the salary impact will be zero.		
Pay Raise	+2,666	+3,718
The change reflects the salary impact of a programmed one percent pay raise as proposed in the Circular A-11.		
Employer Share of Federal Health Benefit Plans	+197	+273
The change reflects expected increases in employer's share of Federal Health Benefit Plans.		
Departmental Working Capital Fund	+95	+217
The change reflects expected changes in the charges for centrally billed Department services and other services through the Working Capital Fund. These charges are displayed in the Budget Justification for Department Management.		
Rental Payments	+54	+2
The adjustment is for changes in the costs payable to General Services Administration (GSA) and others resulting from changes in rates for office and non-office space as estimated by GSA, as well as the rental costs of other currently occupied space. These costs include building security; in the case of GSA space, these are paid to Department of Homeland Security (DHS). Costs of mandatory office relocations, i.e. relocations in cases where due to external events there is no alternative but to vacate the currently occupied space, are also included.		

APPROPRIATION: WILDLAND FIRE MANAGEMENT

Appropriations Language

Department of the Interior
(DEPARTMENT-WIDE WILDLAND FIRE PROGRAMS)

WILDLAND FIRE MANAGEMENT
(INCLUDING TRANSFERS)

For necessary expenses for fire preparedness, *fire* suppression operations, fire science and research, emergency rehabilitation, [hazardous] fuels [reduction] *management, resilient landscapes activities*, and rural fire assistance by the Department of the Interior, [$740,982,000] *$793,969,000* to remain available until expended, of which not to exceed $6,127,000 shall be for the renovation or construction of fire facilities: *Provided*, That such funds are also available for repayment of advances to other appropriation accounts from which funds were previously transferred for such purposes: [*Provided further*, That of the funds provided $145,024,000 is for hazardous fuels reduction activities: *Provided further*, That of the funds provided $16,035,000 is for burned area rehabilitation]: *Provided further, That of the funds provided, $268,560,000 is an amount for wildfire suppression operations to meet the terms of section 251(b)(2) of the Balanced Budget and Emergency Deficit Control Act of 1985, as amended, and $240,440,000 is additional new budget authority for wildfire suppression operations specified for purposes of section 251(b)(2) of such Act: Provided further*, That persons hired pursuant to 43 U.S.C. 1469 may be furnished subsistence and lodging without cost from funds available from this appropriation: *Provided further*, That notwithstanding 42 U.S.C. 1856d, sums received by a bureau or office of the Department of the Interior for fire protection rendered pursuant to 42 U.S.C. 1856 et seq., protection of United States property, may be credited to the appropriation from which funds were expended to provide that protection, and are available without fiscal year limitation: *Provided further*, That using the amounts designated under this title of this Act, the Secretary of the Interior may enter into procurement contracts, grants, or cooperative agreements, for [hazardous] fuels [reduction] *management and resilient landscapes* activities, and for training and monitoring associated with such [hazardous] fuels [reduction] *management and resilient landscapes activities*, on Federal land, or on adjacent non-Federal land for activities that benefit resources on Federal land: *Provided further*, That the costs of implementing any cooperative agreement between the Federal Government and any non-Federal entity may be shared, as mutually agreed on by the affected parties: *Provided further*, That notwithstanding requirements of the Competition in Contracting Act, the Secretary, for purposes of [hazardous] fuels [reduction] *management and resilient landscapes* activities, may obtain maximum practicable competition among: (1) local private, nonprofit, or cooperative entities; (2) Youth Conservation Corps crews, Public Lands Corps (Public Law 109-154), or related partnerships with State, local, or nonprofit youth groups; (3) small or micro-businesses; or (4) other entities that will hire or train locally a significant percentage, defined as 50 percent or more, of the project workforce to complete such contracts: *Provided further*, That in implementing this section, the Secretary shall develop written guidance to field units to ensure accountability and consistent application of the authorities provided herein: *Provided further*, That funds appropriated under this heading may be used to reimburse the United States Fish and Wildlife Service and the National Marine Fisheries Service for the costs of carrying out their responsibilities under the Endangered Species Act of 1973 (16 U.S.C.

1531 et seq.) to consult and conference, as required by section 7 of such Act, in connection with wildland fire management activities: *Provided further*, That the Secretary of the Interior may use wildland fire appropriations to enter into leases of real property with local governments, at or below fair market value, to construct capitalized improvements for fire facilities on such leased properties, including but not limited to fire guard stations, retardant stations, and other initial attack and fire support facilities, and to make advance payments for any such lease or for construction activity associated with the lease: *Provided further*, That the Secretary of the Interior and the Secretary of Agriculture may authorize the transfer of funds appropriated for wildland fire management, in an aggregate amount not to exceed $50,000,000, between the Departments when such transfers would facilitate and expedite wildland fire management programs and projects: *Provided further*, That funds provided for wildfire suppression shall be available for support of Federal emergency response actions: *Provided further*, That funds appropriated under this heading shall be available for assistance to or through the Department of State in connection with forest and rangeland research, technical information, and assistance in foreign countries, and, with the concurrence of the Secretary of State, shall be available to support forestry, wildland fire management, and related natural resource activities outside the United States and its territories and possessions, including technical assistance, education and training, and cooperation with United States and international organizations [:*Provided further*, That of the funds made available under section 135 of Public 113-46, $7,500,000 are rescinded and the remaining balances shall not be subject to the pro rata replenishment requirements in section 102 of title I of this division]. (Department of the Interior, Environment, and Related Agencies Appropriations Act, 2014.)

Proposed Change: [hazardous] fuels [reduction] *management,*

Justification: The change to the appropriation language removes the word "hazardous and reduction" from the program name and adds management as a part of the changed title.

Proposed Deletion: [*Provided further,* That of the funds provided $145,024,000 is for hazardous fuels reduction activities: *Provided further,* That of the funds provided $16,035,000 is for burned area rehabilitation]:

Justification: The language applied to 2014, and does not carry forward in 2015. The proposed change provides more flexibility to the Department in the management of WFM resources.

Proposed Addition: "*Provided further,* That of the funds provided $268,560,000 is an amount for wildfire suppression operations to meet the terms of section 251(b)(2) of the Balanced Budget and Emergency Deficit Control Act of 1985, as amended, and $240,440,000 is additional new budget authority for wildfire suppression operations specified for purposes of section 251(b)(2) of such Act:"

Justification: the budget amends the Balanced Budget and Emergency Deficit Control Act to add an adjustment to the discretionary spending limits for wildfire suppression operations. The 2015 budget proposes a new framework for budgeting for wildfire suppression needs in which a portion of the funding need for suppression response is funded within the discretionary spending caps ($268,560,000) and a portion is funded in a budget cap adjustment ($240,440,000).

Proposed Change: "*Provided further,* That using the amounts designated under this title of this Act, the Secretary of the Interior may enter into procurement contracts, grants, or cooperative agreements, for [hazardous] fuels [reduction] *management and resilient landscapes* activities, and for training and monitoring associated with such [hazardous] fuels [reduction] *management and resilient landscapes activities,*"

Justification: The language change in each place it occurs is to acknowledge the name change of Hazardous Fuels Reduction to Fuels Management and add the new Resilient Landscape activity to the overall program.

Proposed Change: [:*Provided further,* That of the funds made available under section 135 of Public 113-46, $7,500,000 are rescinded and the remaining balances shall not be subject to the pro rata replenishment requirements in section 102 of title I of this division]

Justification: The language applied to 2014, and does not carry forward in 2015.

ACTIVITY: WILDLAND FIRE PREPAREDNESS

Preparedness

Activity: Preparedness						
Subactivity: Preparedness						
			FY 2015			
$000	2013 Actual	2014 Enacted	Fixed Costs & Related Changes	Program Changes (+/-)	Request	Change from 2014 (+/-)
Preparedness	264,833	281,928	+2,947	+34,095	318,970	+37,042
FTE	2,277	2,277		+131	2,408	+131

Summary of 2015 Program Changes for Preparedness

Request Component	($000)	FTE
• BIA Tribal Contract and Admin Support	+9,000	+8
• BIA Workforce Development	+6,000	+41
• Maintain Veterans Crews	+1,700	+45
• Firefighter and Support Personnel	+5,395	+37
• Aviation Program Contracts	+10,000	-
• Equipment Capitalization	+2,000	-
TOTAL Program Changes	**+34,095**	**+131**

Justification of 2015 Program Changes

The 2015 budget for the Preparedness program within the WFM program is $319.0 million and 2,408 FTE. This amount includes $2.9 million for fixed costs. This request includes a $34.1 million program change that will strengthen DOI Preparedness capability through aviation program efficiencies, support of a program for hiring returning veterans as firefighting crews, restoration of critical mid-level fire line supervisors and line firefighters, replacement of fire engines and firefighting equipment fleet that exceed their functional life, providing contract and administrative support for the Bureau of Indian Affairs (BIA) and Tribal managed firefighting organizations, and investments in BIA and Tribal workforce development. The total requested program increase includes $15.0 million for the tribal resource management to strengthen BIA and tribal fire management capabilities. Details and justifications of the specific components of the Preparedness request follow.

BIA Tribal Contract and Admin Support (+$9,000/ +8 FTE) – The BIA wildland fire management program is required to pay contract support costs to Tribes for tribal management of contracted and compacted wildland fire management programs. These costs have historically been paid from BIA's allocation of Preparedness funds, which reduces funds intended for program management and oversight, wildfire prevention, wildfire detection, and wildfire response readiness. Contract support costs have continued to increase in Indian Country, as wildland fire management moves from BIA managed programs to a greater number of Self-Government compacts, Public Law 93-638 contracts, or cooperative agreement wildland fire programs managed by the Tribes. This component of tribal resource management will provide the necessary contract support funding for BIA to support the Tribal-managed firefighting organizations, which is a complex process. This request will also provide administrative support funding to implement standardized business practices, enhance technical assistance to Tribes in WFM financial management, allow more timely processing of tribal invoices, allow more timely allocation of program funds to operational units, improve communication of budget status with internal/external budget customers, and allow fire management officers to focus on operational duties rather than administrative tasks.

BIA Workforce Development (+$6,000/ +41 FTE) - This component for tribal resource management will be used for workforce development. Many of the BIA's firefighters currently are part-time Administratively Determined (AD) Emergency Fire Fighters (EFF) paid from the Suppression account. This initiative will develop steady, long-term employment opportunities for American Indian and Alaska Native youths, while reducing dependence on the AD workforce. In addition, this initiative will provide education, training and leadership development for these new employees.

Maintain Veterans Crews (+$1,700/ +45 FTE) – Veteran hiring and the transition of our troops back to civilian careers is a priority for the Department. The hiring of veterans for wildland fire is a natural fit and is a part of the program. Veterans can bring knowledge in leadership, teamwork, operational planning, perseverance under stress, and other qualities that are highly applicable to the wildland firefighting environment. The requested funding will support maintaining four 20-person hand crews resulting in jobs for 80 returning veterans.

Firefighter and Support Personnel (+$5,395 / +37 FTE) – This increase will allow Interior to add approximately 70-80 critical mid-level fire line supervisors and line firefighters to strengthen our initial and extended attack capability. Adding these positions also enhances the fire program's leadership development pipeline.

Aviation Program Contracts (+$10,000 / 0 FTE) – This requested funding increase will enable DOI to fund six Type-3 helicopters and one Type-2 helicopter, and to convert three Type-3 helicopters to Type-2 helicopters. The conversion of Type-3 to Type-2 helicopters will increase the aviation program's ability to transport crews and cargo, and also increase the aviation fleet's water-carrying capabilities. In addition, the Department will fund additional exclusive use Single Engine Air Tankers (SEAT) contracts (eliminating routine use of call-when-needed contracts) and centralize the management of those contracts.

Equipment Capitalization (+$2,000/ 0 FTE) – Some bureaus' fire engine and firefighting equipment was not replaced timely and has now exceeded the useable life. To increase efficiency in managing the replacement of firefighting equipment and to create a safer, more dependable wildland fire fleet, the Department will use the requested increase to buy replacement engines for the Fish and Wildlife Service fire program. These engines will be managed under the Bureau of Land Management's WCF. This change will result in more efficient management of the Department's engine and equipment fleet, increase dependability and safety, and avoids creating a duplicative administrative management organization. This proposal expands the interagency WCF efficiency that has existed between BLM and National Park Service wildfire management programs for several years.

Program Overview

The Preparedness program contributes toward the DOI Strategic Plan's Mission Area #1, Goal #1, and Strategy #3 by managing fire to provide for public and firefighter safety in wildfire response. *"Respond to Wildfires"* is one of three goals identified in the National Cohesive Wildland Fire Management Strategy (Cohesive Strategy). The other two goals are to *"Maintain Resilient Landscapes"* and *"Creating Fire-Adapted Communities"*. The WFM Preparedness program provides the capability to effectively and cost-efficiently respond to wildfires to meet protection objectives, and provide for public and firefighter safety.

The WFM mission includes protecting property and natural and cultural resources from the detrimental effects of wildfires while providing for firefighter and public safety. The WFM program funds Preparedness activities on more than 500 million acres of public lands. The Interior bureaus carry out wildfire response in national parks, wildlife refuges and preserves, Indian reservations and tribal lands, and on other public lands. These diverse lands include historic and cultural sites, commercial forests, rangelands, and valuable wildlife habitat, as well as some lands managed by other Federal and State agencies.

Fire prevention, readiness, and wildfire response programs are implemented by Federal fire crews, or through cooperative protection agreements with other Federal and State agencies, through self-governing Tribes, and through contracts with private firms and vendors. The bureaus enter into cooperative agreements with other Federal agencies as well as State, tribal, and local governments to leverage resources and gain efficiency and reduce redundancy and duplicative efforts. Under these arrangements, protection responsibilities are exchanged and resources are shared. These cooperative agreements help minimize overall protection costs for all parties and build relationships that are essential to development of a cohesive and coordinated response to managing wildfires, which is especially important when fires burn across land ownerships and multiple jurisdictional wildfire response agencies' administrative boundaries.

Wildland fire management activities within the Department are guided by fire management plans. Fire management plans provide the basis for wildland fire Preparedness staffing and equipment. In the planning process consideration is given to planned contributions from interagency-shared resources, required training, wildfire prevention and detection, as well as land use guidance on appropriate response to wildfires to meet management and protection objectives. Deployment of the Department's wildfire prevention and wildfire response resources are based on these fire management plans, considering current year predicted fire activity, and in coordination with interagency fire cooperators, and State and local wildfire protection authorities.

The WFM program enhances the economic efficiency of the program by pooling DOI's financial resources to provide national-shared fire management resources that are collectively identified through national interagency coordination and collaboration. Such resources include retardant dropping air tankers, retardant bases, lead planes, interagency hotshot crews, smokejumpers, large transport planes, and technical predictive services and meteorological support staffs. In addition to the program's permanent, career-seasonal, and temporary firefighting positions, program management resources include permanent and career-seasonal professional staffs that provide leadership, coordination, program planning, dispatch, warehouse, and other support and logistical functions along with technical and administrative support for fire and aviation management activities. Personnel from non-Preparedness programs (such as Fuels Management and other WFM programs) also support fire suppression activities and, together with Preparedness employees, comprise the Department's core firefighting resources. In addition to the core firefighting resources, a "militia" of other non-WFM funded employees throughout the Department maintains fire qualifications and supports firefighting operations on an as-needed basis.

The Department, in cooperation with the USFS, and the National Weather Service, hosts the National Interagency Fire Center (NIFC) in Boise, Idaho. The NIFC is not an organization, but is a physical location at which a number of coordinated WFM activities take place. The Interior's wildland fire bureaus' program offices reside at NIFC, along with the National Incident Coordination Center (NICC) and certain operational elements. The NICC is an interagency organization that provides long and short-term fire outlook assessments, manages and coordinates national-level firefighting resource mobilization, and tracks and reports on daily wildland fire activity. The NIFC hosts one of 11 national fire caches for supplies and equipment along with the National Incident Radio Cache. Interagency organizations at NIFC coordinate and develop programs and capabilities in support of the WFM program, including communications, remote sensing, wildland fire information technology, and training courses in wildfire suppression and prescribed fire management.

Preparedness program resources include unit-level assets, plus regional and national shared resources such as interagency hotshot crews that are available to fight fires on Federal and non-Federal lands protected under exchange agreements or cooperative agreements. When Federal assistance is requested, these resources may also be used to assist local communities and States on a reimbursable basis. Wildland firefighting resources are mobile and may be moved locally, regionally, or nationally to respond to wildfires. As conditions change during a fire season, or as activity increases in specific locations, mobile firefighting resources are moved to those locations that have the greatest risk and protection needs. Wildfires know no boundaries and typically may involve Federal, State, and local jurisdictions. Interagency cooperation and coordination are essential to effective and efficient wildfire response.

The movement of wildland firefighting resources is coordinated through the National Multi-Agency Coordination group (NMAC) at the NIFC. The NMAC includes representatives from the five Federal wildland fire firefighting agencies, the National Association of State Foresters, and the U.S. Fire Administration. The NMAC utilizes wildfire activity intelligence information collected from 11 Geographic Area Coordination Centers (GACCs) and interviews with their associated Geographic Multi-Agency Coordination Groups (GMACs) representatives. The GACCs collect and consolidate intelligence information on local wildfire activity and response details from local wildfire dispatch centers. If firefighting resources are depleted in a particular local or geographic area, then firefighting units may be mobilized from the next closest local or geographic area or other parts of the country to assist and to meet those wildfire management needs. This mobility of wildland firefighting resources reduces costs and maximizes utilization of valuable firefighting assets. During national wildfire Preparedness Levels 4 and 5, the highest levels of wildfire activity, competition for firefighting resources may occur. During these periods the NMAC evaluates risks and protection needs to prioritize and allocate resources across the Nation.

Through the use of predictive services, wildfire managers evaluate indicators of burn probability, fire potential, and long-term drought, and weather trends to forecast areas that may be subject to increased or severe wildfire activity. When wildfire activity is forecasted to exceed historical norms, wildfire response resources are deployed in advance of fire emergencies. This pre-positioning of wildfire response resources ensures that the Department is ready to efficiently respond when wildfires occur.

The Department is working with the USFS to explore ways to increase our effectiveness in Preparedness and Fuels Management budget formulation and allocation. The DOI is interested in USFS research in the use of wildfire risk assessment to inform Preparedness and Fuels Management budget decisions. The Department is investigating a collaborative risk-based approach based on peer-reviewed science including the use of existing nationally consistent data sets and analysis tools that were developed through the Fire Program Analysis (FPA).

The Fire Program Analysis (FPA) provides decision support information elements to aid in our development of a method for formulating and allocating budgets which ensures funding is used in the most effective manner to reduce risk and improve efficiency.

The focus will be on risks to community values, natural and cultural resources, and identifying the investments that most effectively reduce that risk. The identification of and agreement on the key performance measures that demonstrate the value of investments in Preparedness and Fuels are essential to our continued success.

In FY 2013, the Department completed the Interior Fire Program Assessment to evaluate potential for increased efficiency in management of the WFM program. Based on this study and prior internal analyses, the Department and bureaus have reduced duplication and increased efficiency across the WFM program.

These innovations include the following shared services:
- Working Capital Fund (WCF) support for fire engine fleet management;
- WFM Human Resource services at NIFC, including the recruitment and hiring of seasonal firefighters;
- national payment processing center for Administratively Determined (AD) Emergency Fire Fighters (EFF);
- acquisition and contracting for WFM resources
- DOI Medical Standards program management staff and contract;
- Single Engine Air Tanker (SEAT) contract administration;
- shared national fire planning support;
- Remote Automatic Weather Station (RAWS) program support;
- inter-departmental and interagency managed Wildland Fire Information and Technology (WFIT) portfolio;
- Wildland Fire Decision Support System (WFDSS) center serving all Federal wildland fire agencies;
- interagency initial attack dispatch centers and geographic and national area coordination centers.

Innovations in program delivery include improved management of wildland fire information and technology (IT) projects and data management. The Department and its bureaus have combined with USFS to provide a unified interagency oversight for wildland fire management information technology projects, programs, and data sources. This interagency IT coordination allows staff skills and expertise to be shared across multiple projects and results in less duplication in staff and duplicative IT systems, leverages shared funding, and results in better coordination of desired business needs across agencies. One example of project that has benefited from this cross-agency coordination is the Integrated Reporting of Wildland Fire Information (IRWIN) which links data from 14 different systems, coordinates 70 data elements to reduce multiple data entry in different systems, and reduces the potential for conflicting data across different systems for the same data element. (See discussion on IRWIN below.)

At the local level, more wildfire response organizations are moving toward shared fire staffs through Service First authorities or other agreements, reducing duplication of management and administrative support staffs while maintaining appropriate levels of operational response.

2015 Program Performance

Wildfire response resources are critical to the effective management of wildfires to meet protection and natural and cultural resource management objectives. Federal wildfire management agencies emphasize risk-informed wildfire response that takes aggressive suppression actions when required to protect life, property, and other assets at risk, while minimizing wildfire response actions in areas where risks are low and benefits can be derived from managing wildfires to reduce fuels and future wildfire potential, to meet natural and cultural resource management objectives, or to increase safety by reducing firefighter exposure. This practice of managing wildfires for multiple objectives allows the use of fire management strategies and tactics to manage risk, meet protection and resource objectives, and reduce overall cost.

Effective response to wildfire requires the proper resources to analyze risks, evaluate potential actions, provide program management and program oversight, and provide operational resources necessary to manage wildfires. In 2015, the Department is requesting a $34.1 million program increase to bolster and sustain the Interior's ability to effectively and efficiently respond to wildfires. This program change request is for aviation program efficiencies, support of a program for hiring returning veterans as firefighting crews, restoration of critical mid-level fire line supervisors and line firefighters, replacement of fire engines and firefighting equipment fleet that have exceed their functional life, providing the necessary contract and administrative support for the Bureau of Indian Affairs and Tribal managed firefighting organizations, and to invest in BIA and Tribal workforce development.

Estimated Government Preparedness Resources, FY2013 - FY2015 [1]

Firefighting Asset	Resource Type		FY2013 Enacted	FY2014 Planned	FY2015 Estimated
Personnel	Fire Personnel		3,945	3,945	4,094
		FTE	*2,277*	*2,277*	*2,408*
	Smokejumpers		136	136	136
	Type 1 Crews		16	16	16
Equipment	Engines		728	715	701
	Other Equipment		95	89	85
Aviation	Water Scoopers		3	3	5
	Single Engine Air Tankers		11	13	33
	Helicopters Type 2		7	7	11
	Helicopters Type 3		33	33	31
	Smokejumper		7	7	7
	ASM/Lead plane		4	4	5
	Air Tactical		10	10	11
	Utility		4	4	5

[1] This table is an estimate only. Actual numbers are dependent upon timing and implementation of specific budgetary actions.

Estimated Tribal Preparedness Resources, FY2013 - FY2015 [1]

Firefighting Asset	Resource Type	FY2013 Enacted	FY2014 Planned	FY2015 Estimated
Personnel	Fire Personnel	367	367	367
	Tribal Staff Equivalent	*186*	*186*	*186*
	Type 1 Crews	4	4	4
Equipment	Engines	130	130	130

[1] This table is an estimate only. Actual numbers are dependent upon timing and implementation of specific budgetary actions.

Estimated Preparedness Program Costs ($000) FY2013 - FY2015

General Cost Category	FY2013 Enacted	FY2014 Planned	FY2015 Estimated
Salaries and Benefits	$ 177,098	$ 188,998	$ 205,354
Travel and PCS Move	$ 4,383	$ 4,678	$ 5,257
General Contracts and Agreements	$ 6,776	$ 7,231	$ 9,354
Aviation Contracts	$ 23,612	$ 25,199	$ 35,627
Tribal Contracts and Agreements	$ 21,930	$ 23,404	$ 27,801
Fire Vehicle and Equipment Fleet	$ 8,705	$ 9,290	$ 11,448
Supplies and Materials	$ 12,778	$ 13,362	$ 13,590
Other	$ 9,551	$ 9,766	$ 10,539
Total Program Cost	**$ 264,833**	**$ 281,928**	**$ 318,970**

Integrated Reporting of Wildland-Fire Information

The Integrated Reporting of Wildland-Fire Information (IRWIN) service is a Wildland Fire Information and Technology (WFIT) affiliated investment that is intended to provide an "end–to–end" fire reporting capability. This investment will streamline incident business processes and improve the quality of data for collecting and reporting incidents and events. The IRWIN Core team is tasked with providing integrated data exchange capabilities between the existing applications used to manage incidents related to wildland fire. IRWIN is focused on the goals of reducing redundant data entry, identifying authoritative data sources, and improving the consistency, accuracy, and availability of operational data.

The financial benefits associated with implementing an end-to-end reporting capability with IRWIN are estimated based on different workloads that comprise a significant portion of fire reporting operations and total approximately $394 million in cost savings over a 15-year period; with cost benefits beginning to be realized in Year 5 (estimated to be FY 2018). Workload costs are based upon the time it takes for dispatchers to enter fire incident data, the number and types of fire incidents, and dispatcher labor rates. This data was obtained from the *Interagency Wildland Fire Dispatch and Related Services report, Data Records (October 23, 2008)*.

Evidence to Date: Integration testing when incorporated in five applications and allowed approximately 70 data elements to be entered once and dynamically shared with the wildland fire business incident environment. The test was conducted in Boise, Idaho, with business representatives from the interagency wildland fire community (including federal, state, and local participants). The test proved a time savings of 600 percent in fire business processes. Currently, IRWIN is on target to "go live" in the spring of 2014 and continue on an annual cycle of increasing data exchange by approximately 5 systems per year.

The project discovery and prototyping started in 2011 with a budget of $1.5 million and continued in 2012 with an additional $1.5 million. Funding for FY 2013-2014 and requested in 2015 is $3 million annually.

Program Performance Table – Preparedness

Performance Measure	2010 Actual	2011 Actual	2012 Actual	2013 Actual	2014 Plan	2015 Request	Change from 2014 Plan to 2015
Percent of wildfires on DOI-managed landscapes where the initial strategy(ies) fully succeeded during the initial response phase. (SP)	97%	97%	97%	98%	97%	97%	0%
	(6,480/ 6,655)	(7,527/ 7,770)	(9,175 / 9,454)	(6,330 / 6,482)	(7,360 / 7,580)	(7,370/ 7,600)	(0 / 0)
Percentage of all wildfire not contained in initial attack that exceed a stratified cost index (BUR)	18%	9%	9%	9%	10%	10%	0%

ACTIVITY: SUPPRESSION OPERATIONS

Suppression Operations

Activity: Suppression Operations						
Subactivity: Suppression						
			FY 2015			
$000	2013 Actual	2014 Enacted	Fixed Costs & Related Changes	Program Changes (+/-)	President's Budget	Change from 2014 (+/-)
Suppression	261,206	285,878	0	-17,318	268,560	-17,318
FTE	470	470	0	0	470	0

* 2013 Suppression actual includes repayment of $15.5 million in Section 102 transfers and reductions for sequestration.

Justification of 2015 Program Changes

The 2015 budget for the Suppression Operations program within the Wildland Fire Management (WFM) Appropriation is $268.6 million, a program decrease of $17.3 million and 0 FTE from the 2014 Enacted level. The budget also includes $240.4 million as a budget cap adjustment.

The 2015 budget proposes to amend the Balanced Budget and Emergency Deficit Control Act (BBEDCA) of 1985, as amended, to establish a new budget framework for the WFM program designed to provide stable funding for fire suppression, while minimizing the adverse impacts of fire transfers on the budgets of other fire and non-fire programs, as well as reduce fire risk, manage landscapes more comprehensively, and increase the resiliency of public lands and the communities that border them. In this proposed new budget framework, a portion of the funding need for suppression response is funded within the discretionary spending caps and a portion is funded in a budget cap adjustment. In addition, our request does not increase overall discretionary spending, as it would reduce the available ceiling for the existing disaster relief cap adjustment by an equivalent amount as is provided for wildfire suppression operations.

In FY 2015, 70 percent of the 10-year average is $268.6 million (see following table):

	SUPPRESSION OBLIGATIONS 2004 – 2013 *(Dollars in Thousands)*				
Year	Net Nominal Suppression Obligations	GDP Inflator A/[2005=1.00]	GDP Deflator [2013=1.00]	Adjusted Obligations [2013=1.00]	Rolling 10-Year Avg
2004	281,244	0.9685	0.8109	346,843	293,642
2005	294,054	1.0000	0.8372	351,218	312,685
2006	424,058	1.0331	0.8650	490,267	339,724
2007	470,491	1.0597	0.8872	530,296	378,036
2008	392,783	1.0976	0.9190	427,423	405,493
2009	218,418	1.1036	0.9240	236,389	407,922
2010	231,214	1.1191	0.9370	246,772	387,689
2011	318,788	1.1432	0.9571	333,065	385,686
2012	465,832	1.1711	0.9805	475,100	382,143
2013	399,199	1.1944	1.0000	399,199	383,657

The amount requested in the cap adjustment equals the difference between the total amount of suppression expenditures projected for the fiscal year, based on the Outyear Forecast developed by the U.S. Forest Service's Southern Research Station, and the 70 percent of the 10-year suppression average that is requested within the discretionary budget caps. For 2015, the request for the budget cap adjustment is $240.4 million (see table below):

FY 2015 DOI Suppression Expenditure Forecast and Confidence Interval (CI)
(dollars in thousands)

	Median total DOI Expenditure	Lower 90 Percent CI	Upper 90 Percent CI	FY 2015 Pres. Budget Suppression	FY 2015 Proposed Cap Adjustment
FY 2015	$396,440	$282,180	$508,770	$268,560	$240,440

Funds within the budget cap adjustment will only be accessible for wildland fire suppression operations if one or more of the following criteria are met and a declaration has been issued by the Secretary of the Interior:

   • a fire has required an emergency Federal response based on significant complexity, severity, or threat posed by the fire to human life, property, or resource, or
   • the fire covers 1,000 acres or more, or
   • the fire is within 10 miles of a major urban area (defined as 50,000 inhabitants or more), or

• the cumulative costs of wildfire suppression operations will exceed all of the amounts previously appropriated within 30 days.

Program Overview

The WFM, Suppression Operations activity funds the emergency and unpredictable aspects of the Department's Wildland Fire Management program. Suppression Operations include a range of actions taken to manage wildfires in a safe, cost-effective manner, while protecting values at risk in a manner consistent with resource objectives and land management plans.

Wildfire response actions range from intensive suppression when wildfires on public lands threaten communities, high value resources, or critical ecosystems, to monitoring wildfires in areas where burning accomplishes resource benefits or where it is too dangerous to place firefighters. Emergency stabilization of stream banks and soils is undertaken during and immediately following, a wildfire to reduce the risk of resource damage caused by floods, landslides, and erosion. Emergency stabilization is performed within one year of containment of a wildfire; these projects may be monitored for up to three years after containment.

Supppression Operations program costs include expenses incurred by fireline, command, and support personnel required above those costs covered by Preparedness. The Suppression Operations activity also funds temporary emergency firefighters, aircraft flight operations and support, logistical services, supplies, equipment (including replacement of lost or damaged capital and expendable equipment), contracts for goods and services, administrative support directly associated with incidents, and immediate measures to repair damage as a result of wildfire response activities.

Severity funding, which provides extra preparedness resources in above-normal or extreme conditions, is included in Suppression Operations. Severity funding is used to improve initial response capabilities when abnormal, severe wildfire conditions occur. Abnormal wildfire conditions arise when wildfire seasons start earlier than normal, last longer than normal, or exceed average high fire danger ratings for prolonged periods. Severity funds typically are used to temporarily increase firefighting staff, pay for personnel and equipment, pre-position wildfire response units, conduct additional aerial reconnaissance, and acquire other supplemental contract services. Severity authorizations are subject to strict controls to better manage the expenditure of these funds.

2015 Program Performance

Although DOI's annual Suppression Operations expenditures fluctuate from year to year, the inflation adjusted 10-year average of Suppression obligations has increased by about 31 percent over 2004. This trend is attributable to a number of factors:

- Climate variability has led to increased drought conditions, vegetation conversion (increased flammability and shorter fire return intervals), insect infestations, earlier mountain snow melt, extended burning seasons, increased number of ignitions, and greater wildfire severity.

- Persistent drought and accumulation of flammable fuels has contributed to an increase in the number, size, and severity of large wildfires.

- According to the *2009 Quadrennial Fire Review*, risk levels also increase as a result of population growth and home construction in the WUI and the Intermix[1]. This rapid growth into wildland areas complicates landscape protection needs and creates additional sources of ignition.

To address these factors and others, the Federal fire management agencies are pursuing, implementing and refining strategies and practices aimed at containing firefighting costs. Ongoing efforts at cost containment, the use of risk-based management strategies, including the management of wildfires for multiple objectives in appropriate areas, are contributing to cost efficiencies in wildfire response.

The Department continues to emphasize the use of a risk-based strategy to allow wildfires to be managed for multiple objectives: a single wildfire may be simultaneously suppressed in one spot and allowed to burn for resource benefit in another without contradicting policy. These operations balance the allocation of suppression funding with the risk a wildfire poses to the public or to natural or cultural resources. Tactics can range from aggressive suppression to monitoring low-risk wildfires managed for multiple objectives. The Department is making a concerted effort to allow fire to return to the landscape where fire will improve the health of the land and when risks to safety and communities make it appropriate to do so.

The Department is continuing to work closely with the U.S. Forest Service to further address the challenge of rising suppression costs. A number of positive steps have been taken, including emphasizing land management decisions that affect fuel loading and resource protection, increasing the skills of local firefighters, advancing integrated data management, providing clarification for master cost-sharing agreements, and developing metrics and accountability measures to evaluate managerial cost effectiveness.

---

[1]Interface generally refers to areas with communities near wildland, while Intermix has fewer houses and more vegetation.

Use of Cost and Performance Information in the Suppression Program

- The Department's fire managers continue to prioritize the allocation of funding for initial response capability, a critical step in keeping new fire starts from becoming fires of significance.

- For the Federal wildland fire management agencies, the primary criterion for choosing wildfire response strategies is to minimize costs without compromising safety. Planned and actual suppression costs must be commensurate with the values to be protected. Rationale for suppression expenditures are included and displayed in the Wildland Fire Decision Support System (WFDSS), a web-based tool mandated to be used for all Federal fires that escape initial response. WFDSS allows managers to make informed decisions about incident management considering safety, complexity, risk, and economics.

- Interagency fire management policy stipulates that Incident Business Advisors must be assigned to any fire with costs of $5 million or more. Interagency Large Fire Cost Reviews are conducted when DOI incidents exceed expenditures of $10 million. For the DOI agencies, State/regional directors and bureau directors must approve incident expenditures as they reach key thresholds.

- The Integrated Reporting of Wildland-Fire Information (IRWIN) project will provide an "end–to–end" fire reporting capability that promises to streamline incident business processes and improve the quality of data collected for reporting on incidents and events. IRWIN will reduce redundant data entry across wildland fire information systems, will promote a consistent and repeatable process to gather fire information, and will provide agency personnel with a consolidated view of fire data. IRWIN will make review and analysis of fire suppression incidents and programmatic evaluation of the Suppression Operations activity less cumbersome and more reliable.

Supporting Performance Measures	Type	2010 Actual	2011 Actual	2012 Actual	2013 Actual	2014 Target	2015 Request	Change from 2014 to 2015 Request	Long-Term Target 2018
Strategy #3: Manage wildland fire for landscape resiliency, strengthen the ability of communities to protect against fire, and provide for public and firefighter safety in wildfire response.									
Percent of wildfires on DOI-managed landscapes where the initial strategy (ies) fully succeeded during the initial response phase. (SP)	A	97%	97%	97%	98%	97%	97%	0%	99%

These new performance measures were established in 2014. For implementation of these measures in 2015, a baseline was extrapolated from historical data.

Other Significant Fire Program Measures

Supporting Performance Measures	Type	2010 Actual	2011 Actual	2012 Actual	2013 Actual	2014 Plan	2015 Request	Change from 2014 Plan to 2015	Long-Term Target 2018
Percentage of all fires not contained in initial attack that exceed a stratified cost index(BUR)	A	18%	9%	9%	9%	10%	10%	0%	TBD
Percent change from the 10-year average in the number of acres burned by unplanned and unwanted wildland fires on Interior lands (BUR) %=difference between yearly acres and 10-yr avg. acres.	A	-41% 1,423,895	-38% 1,423,895	37% 3,186,827	-36% 1,570,717	0.0% 2,403,600	18% 2,402,000	18%	0.5% 2,637,182
		(-884,429/ 2,178,975)	(-861,923/ 2,285,818)	(865,740/ 2,321,087)	(-897,056/ 2,467,773)	(3,600/ 2,400,000)	367,000/ 2,035,000		(12,850/ 2,624,332)

Target Codes: SP = Strategic Plan Measure, BUR = Fire Program Specific Measure, HPG = High Performance Goal, NA = Long-Term Targets Inappropriate to Determine At This Time, UNK = Prior Data Not Available

Type Codes: C=Cumulative Measure, A = Annual Measure, F = Future Measure

SUBACTIVITY: FUELS MANAGEMENT

Fuels Management

Activity: Other Operations						
Subactivity: Fuels Management						
			FY 2015			
$000	**2013 Actual**	**2014 Enacted**	**Fixed Costs & Related Changes**	**Program Changes (+/-)**	**Request**	**Change from 2014 (+/-)**
Activity	137,685	145,024	+1,263	+0	146,287	+1,263
FTE	1,013	1,013		+0	1,013	0

Justification of 2015 Program Changes

The 2015 budget for the Fuels Management program within the WFM program is $146.3 million and 1,013 FTE. This is equal to the FY 2014 Enacted level, with an increase of $1.3 million for fixed costs. Within the total, $10.0 million will be directed to support the Tribal resource management landscape restoration, which will fund projects aimed at fulfilling trust responsibilities on reserved treaty rights lands. The program name is formally changed from "Hazardous Fuels Reduction" to "Fuels Management." The management of fuels through the use of prescribed fire, mechanical treatments, and other means is a fundamental component of the overall WFM program.

Program Overview

Accumulations of vegetation, combined with sustained drought, insect infestation, and a changing climate contribute to increased wildfire intensity, spread, and resistance to control throughout many parts of the United States. The management of these wildfires is further compounded by the growth of communities adjacent or within public lands, placing homes and other structures closer to areas where large wildland fires occur. Decades of successful wildfire suppression have led to an increase in fuel accumulation and some areas have become unable to recover from a fire, even in areas where the ecosystem is fire tolerant or even fire dependent. Fuels treatments do not eliminate risks posed by wildfire from our landscapes. They can, however, result in better outcomes for mitigating and managing risk. Fuels treatments provide many benefits to society, including clean water, scenic and recreational values, wood products, and biodiversity. Communities are better able to withstand wildfire. In addition, treatments provide safer conditions and more strategic options for firefighters.

The purpose of the DOI Fuels Management program is to improve the integrity and resilience of our forests and rangelands; contribute to community adaptation to fire; and improve the ability to safely and appropriately respond to wildfire.

The Fuels Management program uses a risk-based approach that focuses on three strategic issues:
- The nature and extent of the fuels problem in terms of risk of wildfire to key values, primarily in the WUI;

- Determination of treatment and funding priorities based on those risks; and
- Measurement of accomplishment and program success in terms of reduction of those risks.

The Fuels Management program continues to support the three goals of the intergovernmental National Cohesive Wildland Fire Management Strategy. The Fuels Management program goals are to:
- Manage fuels to reduce spread, intensity and/or severity of wildfire in order to protect values at risk.
- Restore and maintain resilience of natural systems to wildfire by reducing uncharacteristically high fuel loads, so that when wildfire occurs, ecological impacts are positive or neutral.
- Provide strategic opportunities to increase our capability to manage wildfire for resource benefits.

The Fuels Management program removes or modifies vegetation to restore and maintain healthy, resilient landscapes; reduces wildfire risks to communities and other values by reducing the risk of severe and potentially dangerous wildfire behavior; lessens post-wildfire damage; and limits the spread and proliferation of invasive species and detrimental pathogens. The Fuels Management program collaborates with other programs within the DOI bureaus to implement projects and treatments that remove or modify vegetation for other primary objectives such as wildlife habitat improvement or timber production.

The core Fuels Management program activities include conducting fuels inventories and assessments, ensuring regulatory compliance, preparing sites for treatment, implementing treatments, and monitoring and evaluating completed treatments, which requires a trained, specialized workforce to accomplish. The program emphasizes coordination, cooperation, and collaboration among Federal agencies, State, local, and tribal governments, and other stakeholders. Program efficiencies are encouraged and in place at all organizational levels. Community assistance is provided in the form of community education and collaborative planning.

In 2015, projects will be placed in the highest priority areas, primarily in the WUI, to mitigate the effects of wildfire on the highest priority values, with program emphasis on the goals previous described above.

The Fuels Management program will be aligned with the Resilient Landscape activities and will continue to coordinate with the bureau natural resources programs.

Tribal resource management landscape restoration funding will focus fuels efforts on reserved treaty right lands. Treaties recognize and establish a unique set of rights, benefits, and conditions for Tribes who agree to cede millions of acres of their lands to the United States and accept its protection. Like other treaty obligations of the United States, Indian treaties are considered to be "the supreme law of the land," and are the foundation upon which Federal Indian law and Federal Indian trust relationship are based.

Within the treaty making process, Tribes retained reserved rights to hunt, fish and gather on usual and accustomed grounds, and in some cases have co-management rights with Federal agencies. For many Tribes, the reserved rights areas fall under the management of other Federal agencies. These Federal agencies may not share the Tribes' priorities for fuels management or may not have the funds to manage acres commensurate with tribal goals and objectives for protection of both tribal trust and reserved rights lands. Consequently, it is essential that Tribes have the ability to participate in collaborative projects to improve the management of these lands. The Department will direct $10.0 million of base Fuels Management funds to Tribes for this purpose, separate from the allocation of Fuels Management funds to the BIA.

 **LANDFIRE and WFDSS**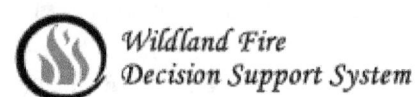

LANDFIRE (Landscape Fire and Resource Management Planning Tools) continues to be a foundational dataset supporting a number of programs within and outside of the WFM program. Within WFM the data products support Preparedness activities and the Fuels Management program by producing consistent national landscape inventory data for supporting decisions in incident management and assisting in the determination of risk from wildfire. LANDFIRE data are an important data set in national and regional level strategic planning, ecological analysis, and decision support.

In FY 2015, LANDFIRE will continue its alignment with the Fuels Management program. LANDFIRE data is also vital to the Preparedness and Suppression Operations activities. For example, LANDFIRE data are used to support the WFDSS. WFDSS is a decision framework used for strategic and tactical planning of fire operations, a critical component of managing long duration fires. LANDFIRE also provides vegetation data layers to non-fire natural resource program managers.

2015 Program Performance

Emphasis will continue to be focused toward the highest priority projects in the highest priority places, and treatments are aimed at mitigating the risk of wildfire to communities and their identified values. The Department is responsible for managing our public lands, refuges, parks, and tribal trust lands, and has concentrated management activities near communities in recent years.

Hazardous Fuels Reduction Spending And Performance	2004 Actual	2005 Actual	2006 Actual	2007 Actual	2008 Actual	2009 Actual D./	2010 Actual D./	2011 Actual	2012 Actual E./	2013 Actual	2014 Planned	2015 Planned
WUI Funding ($000) A/	$ 115,375	$ 132,593	$ 132,302	$ 131,796	$ 148,452	$ 139,643	$ 128,006	$ 164,983	$ 164,719	$ 123,917	$ 87,014	
Acres Treated	490,110	542,568	532,539	586,018	614,319	758,638	696,523	705,274	733,871	471,866	495,500	
Efficiency (Acres/$M)	4,248	4,092	4,025	4,446	4,138	5,433	5,441	4,275	4,455	3,808	5,694	
Cost per Acre	$ 235	$ 244	$ 248	$ 225	$ 242	$ 184	$ 184	$ 234	$ 224	$ 263	$ 176	
Acres Improved B/	UNK	UNK	UNK	212,132	166,491	173,859	174,347	169,032	231,795	191,780	167,400	
Acres Improved/$M	UNK	UNK	UNK	1,610	1,122	1,245	1,362	1,025	571	1,548	1,993	TBD
Acres Improved/Total WUI Acres	UNK	UNK	UNK	36%	27%	23%	25%	24%	32%	41%	34%	
%WUI $	59%	64%	64%	65%	67%	65%	61%	90%	90%	90%	60%	
%WUI Acres	39%	43%	48%	44%	49%	51%	54%	71%	73%	73%	60%	
Non-WUI Funding ($000) A/	$ 80,075	$ 75,282	$ 74,748	$ 71,590	$ 74,730	$ 75,806	$ 80,475	$ 18,331	$ 18,302	$ 13,768	$ 58,010	
Acres Treated	770,797	726,835	573,569	747,404	645,716	742,216	583,297	284,892	266,108	171,318	330,500	
Efficiency (Acres/$M)	9,626	9,655	7,673	10,440	8,641	9,791	7,248	15,542	14,532	12,443	5,697	TBD
Cost per Acre	$ 104	$ 104	$ 130	$ 96	$ 116	$ 102	$ 138	$ 64	$ 69	$ 80	$ 176	
Acres Improved B/	294,000	271,551	241,045	323,806	231,968	194,861	141,606	65,582	102,344	74,139	111,600	
Acres Improved/$M	3,672	3,607	3,225	4,523	3,104	2,571	1,760	3,578	179	5,385	1,924	
Acres Improved/Total Non-WUI Acre	38%	37%	42%	43%	36%	26%	24%	23%	38%	43%	33%	
All Fuels Funding ($000) A/	$ 195,450	$ 207,875	$ 207,050	$ 203,386	$ 223,182	$ 215,449	$ 208,481	$ 183,314	$ 183,021	$ 137,685	$ 145,024	
Acres Treated C./	1,260,907	1,269,403	1,106,108	1,333,422	1,260,035	1,500,854	1,279,820	990,166	999,979	643,184	826,000	
Efficiency (Acres/$M)	6,451	6,107	5,342	6,556	5,646	6,966	6,139	5,401	5,464	4,671	5,696	
Cost per Acre	$ 155	$ 164	$ 187	$ 153	$ 177	$ 144	$ 163	$ 185	$ 183	$ 214	$ 176	TBD
Acres Improved B/	UNK	UNK	UNK	535,938	398,459	368,720	315,953	234,614	334,139	265,919	279,000	
Acres Improved/$M	UNK	UNK	UNK	2,635	1,785	1,711	1,516	1,280	750	1,931	1,924	
Acres Improved/Total Acres	UNK	UNK	UNK	40%	32%	29%	25%	24%	33%	41%	34%	

A./ FY 2004 - 2013 Figures are Actuals; FY 2014 is planned. Actual funds allocated to the projects may vary.

B./ Acres improved are those in fire regimes 1, 2, or 3 moved to a better condition class.

C./Hazardous Fuels Funding only. Landscape restoration (non-National Fire Plan) accomplishments not included.

D./ Includes $10 million in Supplemental HFR funding reprogrammed from Burned Area Rehabilitation accomplishments not included.

E./ FY 2012 and FY 2013 Funds were directed to the WUI (90%) and area immediately adjacent to the WUI (10%). Includes $10 million in Supplemental HFR funding reprogrammed from Burned Area Rehabilitation (242,225 acres). Excludes all ARRA funds and Performance.

Program Performance Table

Goal #1: Protect America's Landscapes

Supporting Performance Measures	Type	2010 Actual	2011 Actual	2012 Actual	2013 Actual	2014 Target	2015 Request	Change from 2014 to 2015 Request	Long-Term Target 2018
Strategy #3: Manage wildland fire for landscape resiliency, strengthen the ability of communities to protect against fire, and provide for public and firefighter safety in wildfire response.									
Percent of DOI-managed treatments that reduce risk to communities that have a wildland fire mitigation plan. (SP)	A	80.1% (4,041/ 5,043)	89.8% (2,648/ 2,949)	93.9% (2,736/ 2,914)	75.6% (1,597/ 2,113)	92.4% (1,570/ 1,700)	93.8% (1,900/ 2,025)	1.4% (330/ 325)	96% (2875/ 3000)

These new performance measures were established in 2014. For implementation of these measures in 2015, a baseline was extrapolated from historical data.

Other Significant Fire Program Measures

Supporting Performance Measures	Type	2010 Actual	2011 Actual	2012 Actual	2013 Actual	2014 Plan	2015 Request	Change from 2014 Plan to 2015	Long-Term Target 2018
Number of high-priority acres treated in the WUI	A	696,523	705,274	733,871	471,866	495,500	TBD	TBD	530,000
Number of acres in fire regimes 1, 2, or 3 moved to a better condition class (WUI & Non-WUI)	A	WUI 174,347 / Non-WUI 141,606 / Total 315,953	WUI 169,032 / Non-WUI 65,582 / Total 234,614	WUI 231,795 / Non-WUI 102,344 / Total 334,139	WUI 191,780 / Non-WUI 74,139 / Total 265,919	WUI 167,400 / Non-WUI 111,600 / Total 279,000	TBD	TBD	WUI 215,000 / Non-WUI 83,000 / Total 298,000
Number of acres in fire regimes 1,2,3 moved to a better condition class per million dollars of gross investment (WUI& non-WUI)	A	WUI 734 / Non-WUI 568 / Total 1,302	WUI 922 / Non-WUI 358 / Total 1,280	WUI 571 / Non-WUI 179 / Total 750	WUI 1,393 / Non-WUI 583 / Total 1,931	WUI 1,154 / Non-WUI 770 / Total 1,924	TBD	TBD	TBD
Number of acres in fire regimes 1, 2, or 3 moved to a better condition class-as a percent of total acres treated (WUI & non-WUI) This is also a long-term measure.	A	WUI 20% / Non-WUI 17% / Total 30%	WUI 17% / Non-WUI 7%, / Total 24%	WUI 23% / Non-WUI 10% / Total 33%	WUI 41% / Non-WUI 43% / Total 41%	WUI 20%, / Non-WUI 14%, / Total 34%	TBD	TBD	TBD

Supporting Performance Measures	Type	2010 Actual	2011 Actual	2012 Actual	2013 Actual	2014 Plan	2015 Request	Change from 2014 Plan to 2015	Long-Term Target 2018
Number of treated acres that are identified in Community Wildfire Protection Plans or other applicable collaboratively developed plans(BUR)	A	594,370	660,673	725,154	368,701	387,000	387,000	0	576,000
Percent of treated acres that are identified in Community Wildfire Protection Plans or other applicable collaboratively developed plans (BUR)	A	(594,370/ 696,523) 85%	(660,673/ 705,274) 94%	(725,154/ 733,871) 99%	(389,919/ 471,866) 83%	(470,725/ 495,500) 95%	(470,725/ 495,500) 95%	0%	(576,000/ 600,000) 96%
Number of acres in WUI treated per million dollars gross investment(BUR)	A	696,523/ $127 M = 5,479	705,274/ $164.98 M = 4,275	733,871/ $132.340 M = 5,545	471,866/ $130.09 M = 3,627	495,500 $87.0M =5,695	TBD	TBD	TBD

Target Codes: SP = Strategic Plan Measure, BUR = Fire Program Specific Measure, HPG = High Performance Goal, NA = Long-Term Targets Inappropriate to Determine At This Time, UNK = Prior Data Not Available

Type Codes: C=Cumulative Measure, A = Annual Measure, F = Future Measure

SUBACTIVITY: RESILIENT LANDSCAPES

Resilient Landscapes

Activity: Other Operations						
Subactivity: Resilient Landscapes						
			FY 2015			
$000	**2013 Actual**	**2014 Enacted**	**Fixed Costs & Related Changes**	**Program Changes (+/-)**	**Request**	**Change from 2014 (+/-)**
Activity	0	0	+0	+30,000	30,000	+30,000
FTE	0	0		+0	0	0

Justification of 2015 Program Changes

The 2015 budget includes $30 million and 0 FTE for Resilient Landscapes within the Department's WFM program. The new Resilient Landscapes program will strengthen the WFM program's ability to contribute to the Cohesive Strategy goal of restoring and maintaining fire-resilient landscapes. Recognizing the cross-cutting benefits of treating fire-adapted ecosystems for land health objectives, the program will provide the opportunity to target specific landscapes, including areas outside the WUI, and enhance integration of these activities between fire and non-fire programs toward shared restoration and ecological objectives.

Program Overview

Landscape resilience is the ability of a landscape to absorb the effects of fire by maintaining or regaining desirable land health characteristics, including its structural, compositional, and functional attributes. Land resiliency is contingent on both the WFM program and the resource management programs. Recognizing the crosscutting, landscape-scale nature of the goal to restore and maintain fire resilient landscapes, program activities will be coordinated with the resource management program activities of the DOI land management bureaus, and projects will receive matching funds from the bureaus. In addition, restoring landscape resiliency and achieving land health objectives has contributing benefits to the WFM program goals of promoting fire-adapted communities and responding to wildfire.

The program will focus on addressing broad land-health outcomes in fire-adapted ecosystems. Activities will be designed to contribute toward longer-term, landscape-scale objectives. Resilient Landscapes funding provides for treatments that improve the integrity and resilience of forests and rangelands by restoring natural vegetation landscapes to a specific condition. Treatments will be strategically placed within priority landscapes where ecosystem structure and function is at elevated risk posed by wildfire to critical natural resources. Priority landscapes will be determined based on an interdisciplinary assessment of where critical resource values are at high risk from wildfire and where the benefits of achieving a condition that is more biologically and ecologically resilient is sustainable in the long-term.

FY 2015 serves as the first year of this new effort for the WFM program. The WFM Fuels Management will work with the bureau natural resource programs for planning, implementation, and monitoring of treatments funded through the Resilient Landscapes subactivity. The WFM program, in coordination with the bureau natural resource programs, will begin determining criteria for achieving landscape resiliency outcomes, completing initial assessments for prioritizing landscapes, soliciting proposals for conducting coordinated activities in priority landscapes, selecting proposals based on the outcomes they will achieve, and determining reporting mechanisms for demonstrating outcome-based performance.

2015 Program Performance

An integrated, risk-based prioritization system for determining priorities will be used. The specific criteria and performance measures for Resilient Landscapes are under development.

Program Performance Table

To be determined

SUBACTIVITY: BURNED AREA REHABILITATION

Burned Area Rehabilitation

			FY 2015			
Activity: Other Operations						
Subactivity: Burned Area Rehabilitation						
$000	**2013 Actual**	**2014 Enacted**	**Fixed Costs & Related Changes**	**Program Changes (+/-)**	**Request**	**Change from 2014 (+/-)**
BAR	12,341	16,035	0	+2,000	18,035	+2,000
FTE	50	45	0	0	45	0
* Note: FTE within the Burned Area Rehabilitation program are not base funded and vary from year to year based on the number of projects, use of contractors versus agency crews, and other variable factors.						

Justification of 2015 Program Changes

The 2015 budget request for the Burned Area Rehabilitation (BAR) program within WFM is $18.0 million and 45 FTE. This represents a program increase of $2.0 million above the 2014 Enacted level.

Program Increase   (+$2,000,000 / 0 FTE)

The budget proposes a program increase of $2.0 million to expand the number of projects to be completed in 2015. The severity of recent wildfires has impacted critical habitat throughout western states, such as the greater sage grouse habitat in the Great Basin. The increase helps address rehabilitation activities needed in response to the 2014, 2013, and 2012 fire seasons.

2015 Program Overview

The BAR program protects resources by maintaining proper function in watersheds and landscapes, and by beginning the recovery of fire-damaged lands. These objectives are achieved by such actions as reseeding to control invasive species, maintaining soil productivity, rehabilitating tribal trust resources, repairing wildlife habitat, and repairing minor facilities damaged by wildfire.

Landscapes that are threatened from post-fire floods or debris flows, or are susceptible to serious degradation, are assessed and treated by the Emergency Stabilization (ES) program within the

Rim Fire, Yosemite National Park

Suppression Operations account up to the first year after a fire. The BAR program provides for longer-term actions to repair damages caused by catastrophic wildfire. Rehabilitation treatments are designed to repair or improve lands unlikely to recover naturally from severe wildfire damage.

The budget for the BAR program is allocated among the WFM bureaus through a rigorous, competitive scoring process based on priorities set by the Department. The local administrative units of the various agencies develop and submit rehabilitation plans for lands damaged by wildfire. These plans are approved by the local agency administrator and then serve as funding requests to agencies and the Department. Recommended project plans are reviewed, scored, and ranked by an interagency team and funding recommendations for the highest priority projects are made by the team. Department and bureau officials subsequently approve projects before final funding allocations are made.

Rehabilitation treatments funded by this program may build upon ES measures and may continue to be implemented up to three years from containment of the fire. After three years, the bureaus' resource management programs assume responsibility for further landscape restoration and monitoring in accordance with land use plans and mission goals.

2015 Program Performance

The primary program goals are the rehabilitation of lands degraded by wildfire. Actual rehabilitation treatments conducted each year are dependent upon the severity of the previous fire seasons, as well as rehabilitation needs required by the damaged resources on the ground. The DOI WFM bureaus will continue to work cooperatively with the USFS, the U.S. Geological Survey, and other scientific institutions to implement monitoring protocols and methods to more accurately assess the effectiveness of wildfire rehabilitation treatments.

The WFM program established a baseline in 2009 to begin measurement of the long-term goal of rehabilitating treated acres to their desired conditions. The description of desired condition includes measurable objectives for physical, chemical, hydrologic, and biologic attributes. Specific measurable objectives may include examples such as managing for specific species composition, canopy cover or vegetation height.

**Use of Cost and Performance Information in the
Burned Area Rehabilitation Program**

To ensure that the highest priority needs are being met first and that funds are used in a consistent manner across the Department. DOI has been using a rigorous process to rank BAR project proposals and allocate funds since 2008. This process will continue in 2015.

This process evaluates the projects against established criteria addressing issues of significant degraded resources and performance. Scores are generated and projects ranked according to their scores.

The results of the scoring produce a ranked list of funded treatments or activities.

Program Performance Table – Burned Area Rehabilitation

Supporting Performance Measures	Type	2010 Actual	2011 Actual	2012 Actual	2013 Actual	2014 Plan	2015 Request	Change from 2014 Plan to 2015	Long-Term Target 2018
End Outcome: Improve Health of Watersheds, Landscapes, and Marine Resources									
Number of treated burned acres that achieve the desired condition (BUR)	A	1,053,945	1,037,658	902,060	4,549,230	1,350,000	1,960,000	610,000	TBD
Percent of treated burned acres that have achieved the desired condition (BUR)	A	95% (1,053,945/ 1,110,844)	97% (1,037,658/ 1,067,892)	88% (1,798,822/ 2,053,270)	87% (4,549,230/ 5,249,050)	90% (1,350,000/ 1,500,000)	89% (1,960,000/ 2,200,000)	-1%	TBD

Comment: A = Annual Measure, NA = Long-Term Targets Inappropriate to Determine At This Time

SUBACTIVITY: FACILITIES CONSTRUCTION AND MAINTENANCE

Facilities Construction and Maintenance

Activity: Other Operations						
Subactivity: Facilities Construction and Maintenance						
			FY 2015			
$000	**2013 Actual**	**2014 Enacted**	**Fixed Costs & Related Changes**	**Program Changes (+/-)**	**Request**	**Change from 2014 (+/-)**
Facilities Construction and Deferred Maintenance	5,806	6,127	0	0	6,127	0
FTE	0	0	0	0	0	0

Justification of 2015 Program Changes

The 2015 budget for the Facilities Construction and Maintenance program is $6.1 million and 0 FTE, which is equal to the FY 2014 Enacted level.

Program Overview

The Facilities Construction and Maintenance Program provide safe, functional, and energy efficient facilities that are essential to the Department's mission to protect lives, property, and resources from wildfire.

The Wildland Fire Management (WFM) program has developed a five-year deferred maintenance and capital improvement plan. The plan presents the projects of greatest need in priority order, focusing first on critical health and safety work, then critical resource protection, energy and building sustainability, critical mission, and code compliance. Each project is submitted according to Departmental guidance for deferred maintenance and capital improvement. To ensure an efficient allocation of funding to the highest priority projects, an interagency team at the NIFC reviews submitted projects by total project score and forwards a prioritized list to the Interior Fire Directors for their recommendation to the Department for approval.

The emphasis areas for the Facilities Construction and Maintenance Program include:

- Correction of critical health and safety-related facility problems to ensure facilities are compliant with federal accessibility requirements and OSHA requirements.
- Installation of facilities that improve the suppression wildfire response capability required to keep fires small and reduce the threat to communities, structures, municipal watersheds, other infrastructure, and wildlife habitat.
- Sufficient fire facilities that allow the program to maintain readiness and provide full support for fire management activities.

Safe and properly maintained facilities are important for protecting firefighters and the equipment upon which they rely. The WFM program is repairing and updating facilities that are in deteriorating and unsafe condition to meet current health and safety standards. Work is accomplished through the authorities of *Public Law 93-638* contracts, *Public Law 297-100* grant processes, or through commercial contracting.

Maintaining a Fire Facilities Construction and Maintenance account separate from the bureaus' Construction and Deferred Maintenance accounts is critical to ensuring effective and efficient fire operations. The program depends on its network of infrastructure, including bunk houses, fire stations, warehouses, and dispatch centers, to support fire crews. These facilities also assist in recruiting firefighters into communities with limited housing, supporting the program's ability to recruit and retain qualified firefighters.

Maintaining a separate fire facilities account also allows the fire program to centrally evaluate projects submitted by all four wildland fire bureaus, enhances coordination, and helps ensure the most cost-efficient allocation of funds to best advance the facility needs of the WFM program's integrated fire program. As facilities are replaced or upgraded, efficiencies in design translate to lower operating costs and energy use, reducing agencies' carbon footprint. The emphasis on energy conservation and sustainability is a major area of importance for all projects.

2015 Program Performance

In 2015, the planned accomplishments in the program include ten projects in six states with the highest critical health, safety, and resource protection ratings at a total cost of $6.1 million. The following table lists the projects that will be funded in 2015.

2015 WILDLAND FIRE CONSTRUCTION
DEFERRED MAINTENANCE PLAN SUMMARY

PROJECT DESCRIPTION	STATE	BUREAU	INTERIOR SCORE	COSTS	INTERIOR RANK
Montrose Fire Station Restoration	CO	BLM	100	919,000	1
Lower Brule Fire Mgmt. Office/Engine Bays Replacement (Phase 2 of 2)	SD	BIA	90	1,750,000	2
McDermitt Fire Station Repair	NV	BLM	90	162,000	3
Winnemucca SEAT Base Repair	NV	BLM	90	68,000	4
Dayville Fire Station Repair	OR	BLM	80	754,000	5
Frenchglen Guard Station Repair	OR	BLM	80	100,000	6
Hackberry Fire Bunkhouse Replacement	NE	FWS	76	600,000	7
Lake Mead Wildland Fire Base Replacement (Phase 1 of 2)	NV	NPS	72	877,000	8
Rydell Engine Storage Renovation	MN	FWS	70	69,000	9
Vale Dispatch Floor Renovation	OR	BLM	60	194,000	10
Architectural and Engineering Design		DOI		634,000	11
TOTAL 2015				**6,127,000**	

Design and construction of all Facilities Construction and Maintenance program projects are monitored by the Department and the bureaus to ensure they are completed within scope and budget. DOI bureaus jointly evaluate departmental project priorities on an annual basis. Out-year priorities are adjusted and updated based on objective criteria applied during the annual evaluation process.

Program Performance Table

	2011 Actual	2012 Actual	2013 Actual	2014 Plan	2015 Request	Change from 2014 Plan to 2015
Fire facilities projects accomplishments or planned	9	7	5	6	10	+4

SUBACTIVITY: JOINT FIRE SCIENCE PROGRAM

Joint Fire Science

			FY 2015			
Activity: Other Operations						
Subactivity: Joint Fire Science Program						
$000	**2013 Actual**	**2014 Enacted**	**Fixed Costs & Related Changes**	**Program Changes (+/-)**	**Request**	**Change from 2014 (+/-)**
Joint Fire Science Program	5,675	5,990	0	0	5,990	0
FTE	4	4			4	0

Justification of 2015 Program Changes

The 2015 budget for the Joint Fire Science Program (JFSP) is $6 million and 4 FTE, which is equal to the 2014 Enacted level.

Program Overview

The JFSP was created by Congress in 1998 as an interagency research, development, and applications partnership between DOI and USDA. Funding priorities and policies are set by the JFSP Governing Board, composed of one representative each from the BIA, BLM, FWS, NPS, USGS, and five representatives from the USFS.

JFSP tailors wildland fire research to emerging needs of policy makers and fire managers through an annual cycle of proposal solicitation, review and funding. Open, competitive proposal solicitations and rigorous peer review are hallmarks of JFSP. Results from JFSP projects are regularly used by land managers to plan and implement fuels treatments, support fire management decisions, restore lands affected by fire, and meet regulatory requirements.

Investment portfolio

The JFSP Governing Board has adopted an investment strategy that allocates program funding in a portfolio approach by balancing funding across different types of fire science and science delivery. Specific areas of emphasis, and funds to be dedicated to each, are determined by the Board in response to consultations with organized groups (e.g. National Wildfire Coordinating Group), and structured interactions (e.g. roundtables). For a list of on-going JFSP projects go to http://www.firescience.gov/JFSP_research.cfm and click on the "Ongoing Research" tab.

Lines of work – Complex topics requiring a long-term science investment strategy to ensure results can be synchronized and integrated for application (~25 percent of program funding):
- o Fuels treatment effectiveness

    o Smoke management

<u>Emerging management needs</u> - Short-term topics of high relevance to managers where significant progress can be made in three years or less (~15 percent of program funding):

<u>New science</u> – Topics where investment is needed in fundamental fire science in order to develop future tools for wildland fire and fuels managers (~10 percent of program funding):

<u>Re-measurement</u> – Opportunistic studies that take advantage of previous investments in field experiments to re-measure existing plots (~10 percent of program funding):

<u>Science delivery</u> – Activities that deliver research results directly to wildland fire and fuel managers through both active and passive approaches (~30 percent of program funding):
    o National Knowledge Exchange Network (15 regional consortia)
    o Research summaries (e.g. Fire Science Digests)
    o Website (www.firescience.gov)
    o Social media (Twitter, Facebook, etc.)

The balance of funds (up to 10 percent) is spent on administration, program initiatives, and program and project evaluation.

Collaboration

The JFSP research projects complement and build on other Federal research programs including those in the USFS, USGS, National Oceanic and Atmospheric Administration, National Aeronautics and Space Administration, and others. More than 90 colleges and universities have collaborated on JFSP-sponsored research projects. Collaboration also extends to private non-profit organizations and tribal, State, county, and local governments as well. In all, over 200 organizations have become partners in JFSP-sponsored research.

2015 Program Performance

The JFSP will continue to invest in wildland fire research and technology transfer. Implementation of the JFSP Smoke Science Plan, the Fuels Treatment Science Plan, and full development of the Regional Knowledge Exchange Consortia will proceed as described in the JFSP Investment Strategy.

Program implementation will continue in the areas of performance described above: lines of work, emerging management needs, new science, re-measurement and science delivery. The JFSP Governing Board will incorporate recommendations from the 2013 independent program review, as appropriate. The program will continue to issue competitive announcements, as well as follow-up on results from prior studies.

Program evaluation activities include an ongoing formal assessment of the Knowledge Exchange Network, and a study of the outcomes of JFSP-funded research scheduled for completion in FY 2015.

Program Performance Table

Measure	2011 Actual	2012 Actual	2013 Actual	2014 Plan	2015 Request	Program Change Accruing in 2015	Program Change Accruing in Out-years
Research projects initiated [1]	36	38	30	30	30	0	N/A
Research projects completed[1]	26	40	44	36	38	+2	N/A
Refereed publications completed[1]	36	49	42	45	45	0	N/A
Science delivery projects completed[2]	25	46	40	n/a	n/a	n/a	N/A
Social media contacts[2]	n/a	n/a	6,315	6,500	6,500	0	N/A
Events/activities[2]	n/a	n/a	1,173	1,200	1,200	0	N/A

[1] JFSP projects are typically completed and published 3-5 years after initiation.
[2] JFSP has expanded its science delivery program by establishing a national network of science exchange partnerships. In FY 2013, in lieu of reporting the number of 'science delivery projects', JFSP began tracking and reporting accomplishments in two sub-categories: events/activities and social media.

For a list of recently completed projects go to http://www.firescience.gov/JFSP_research.cfm and click on the "Completed Research" tab.

APPROPRIATION: FLAME WILDFIRE SUPPRESSION RESERVE FUND

Appropriations Language
FLAME Wildfire Suppression Reserve Fund

(INCLUDING TRANSFER OF FUNDS)

~~For necessary expenses for large fire suppression operations of the Department of the Interior and as a reserve fund for suppression and Federal emergency response activities, $92,000,000, to remain available until expended: *Provided*, That such amounts are only available for transfer to the "Wildland Fire Management" account following a declaration by the Secretary in accordance with section 502 of the FLAME Act of 2009 (43 U.S.C. 1748a).~~ *(Department of the Interior, Environment, and Related Agencies Appropriations Act, 2014.)*

Proposed Change: The FLAME appropriation language is deleted in its entirety.

Justification: In 2015, the Budget proposes to eliminate this account and will fund all suppression activities in the Wildland Fire Management account, with a portion of the suppression funds requested within the discretionary budget cap and a portion of the funds requested in a budget cap adjustment.

Summary of Requirements

(dollars in thousands)

$000	2013 Actual	2014 Enacted	FY 2015			Change from 2014 (+/-)
			Fixed Costs & Related Changes	Program Changes (+/-)	Budget Request	

Activity: FLAME Wildfire Suppression Reserve Fund
Subactivity: Suppression

$000	2013 Actual	2014 Enacted	Fixed Costs & Related Changes	Program Changes (+/-)	Budget Request	Change from 2014 (+/-)
FLAME Wildland Fire Suppression Operations	91,669	92,000	0	-92,000	0	-92,000
FTE	0	0	0	0		0

Justification of 2015 Program Changes

The 2015 budget request for the FLAME Wildfire Suppression Reserve Fund is $0 and 0 FTE, a net program decrease of -$92,000,000 and 0 FTE from the 2014 Enacted level.

Account Elimination   **(-$92,000,000 / 0 FTE)**

No funding is requested for the FLAME account in FY 2015. The Wildland Fire Management discretionary request provides suppression funding equal to 70 percent of the ten year average, which reflects the level of spending associated with suppression of 99 percent of wildfires. In addition, the Budget includes up to $240.4 million to be available under a disaster funding cap adjustment to meet suppression needs above the base appropriation.

Program Overview

The 2010 Interior Appropriations bill established the FLAME Wildfire Suppression Reserve Fund in the Departments of the Interior and Agriculture for the most severe, complex, and threatening fires, and to serve as a contingency reserve. FLAME Funds are currently available to the Secretary of the Interior for transfer into the WFM Suppression Operations account when those funds were nearly exhausted, or when certain objective criteria were met as described in the FLAME Act.

Under the current approach for funding suppression, funds in the FLAME Fund may be transferred from the FLAME Wildfire Suppression Reserve Fund upon a declaration by the Secretary of the Interior or the Secretary of Agriculture. Declarations are based on specific protocols and criteria or when the Suppression account is nearly exhausted. As fires escape initial response, and as Type 1 or Type 2 Incident Management teams are assigned to those escaped incidents, risk assessments and formal risk decisions are made. This decision documentation is part of the declaration for a request to the Secretary of Interior to move funds from the FLAME Act account into the Suppression account. A number of analytical tools such as WFDSS, Fire Spread Probability (FSPro), which models fire behavior, and Rapid Assessment of Values-At-Risk (RAVAR), which models values at risk from fire, provide real-time support to leadership implementing risk-informed management.

Protocols and Objective Criteria

The FLAME Act account functions as a transfer account to accommodate those large wildfires that historically have resulted in the greatest expenditure of Suppression funds. The FLAME Act identifies specific criteria that must be met in order for FLAME Act funds to be transferred to the Suppression account. These include complexity of wildfire incidents, such as assignment of Type 1 or Type 2 Incident Management Teams, or when the regular Suppression account is nearly exhausted. Both of these instances require a declaration by the Secretary, who would then approve the transfer of funds from the FLAME Act account into the Suppression account.

Program Performance

In FY 2013, the Secretary approved the transfer of $91.7 million from the FLAME Fund. Overall, in 2013 there were 179 wildland fires, including 24 on Interior land and 155 on Forest Service land, eligible for FLAME funding due to their severity and the threat they posed to public safety and property. These wildfires exceeded 300 acres in size and were sufficiently complex, as documented in complexity analyses, to warrant the assignment of a Type 1 or Type 2 Incident Management Team (IMT) or National Incident Management Organization (NIMO).

In 2014, the Department will continue to use the FLAME Fund to ensure resources are available for suppression activities when Suppression Operations funds are exhausted and/or appropriate criteria are met.

For more information on the 2015 request, please refer to Suppression Operations section.

EMPLOYEE COUNT BY GRADE

Office of the Secretary - Office of Wildland Fire

Employee Count by Grade
(Total Employment)

	2013 Actuals	2014 Estimate	2015 Estimate
Executive Level V	0	0	0
SES	1	1	1
Subtotal	**1**	**1**	**1**
SL - 00	0	0	0
ST - 00	0	0	0
Subtotal	**0**	**0**	**0**
GS/GM -15	4	4	4
GS/GM -14	12	12	12
GS/GM -13	3	5	5
GS -12	2	2	2
GS -11	2	2	2
GS -10	0	0	0
GS - 9	1	0	0
GS - 8	0	0	0
GS - 7	0	0	0
GS - 6	0	0	0
GS - 5	0	0	0
GS - 4	0	0	0
GS - 3	0	0	0
GS - 2	0	0	0
GS - 1	0	0	0
Subtotal	**24**	**25**	**25**
Other Pay Schedule Systems	0	0	0
Total employment (actuals & estimates)	**25**	**26**	**26**

SECTION 404 COMPLIANCE

Section 404 Compliance - Wildland Fire Management

Description of Program Assessment

($000)

External Administrative Costs	Bureau	Preparedness	Suppression	Fuels	BAR	Basis
Human Resource Fire Program Support	BIA	110	-	-	-	Budget need
Centrally Funded Fire Program Support includes Working Capital Fund Direct and Central bill and BLM Director's Priorities	BLM	4,307	-	1,677	-	% of FTE
National Operations Center (procurement, HR, IT, data management services centrally provided for entire agency)	BLM	921	-	985	-	% of FTE
Headquarters support (general headquarters oversight, external affairs, IT, law enforcement, EEO, HR, resources, business practices)	BLM	656	-	316	-	Evaluation of support needed for subactivity
National Training Center (non-program specific training, centrally funded)	BLM	144	-	57	-	% of FTE
User Pay Cost Share: The non-resource management cost share collects costs from multiple, distributed accounts. The funds collected are used to pay service wide charges that cannot easily be attributed to a specific program or subactivity.	FWS	3,121	-	-	-	% of FTE
Enterprise Wide Cost Share: The Service assesses its resource management programs for costs that can be directly tracked back to users. This includes such items as software licenses, cell phone costs, ID cards and the like.	FWS	263	46	215	14	% of FTE
IT Assessment	NPS	569	-	314	-	% of FTE
Working Capital Fund direct bill - Communications and DOI Access	OS	6	-	-	-	% of FTE
Working Capital Fund central bill - Costs covered include a variety of services including mail services, safety, security, property services, building management and services and finance branch.	OS	313	-	-	-	Share of FTE & square footage.
Subtotal External Administrative		**10,410**	**46**	**3,564**	**14**	

External Administrative Costs

Program Assessments

	Bureau	Preparedness	Suppression	Fuels	BAR	Basis
Reserve Wildland Fire Preparedness & Hazardous Fuels - held to be distributed during mid-year process	OS	100	-	100	-	Reserve
Office of Aircraft Services Central Bill (administrative charges for OAS training, management, flight services, safety)	BLM	-	2,880	-	-	Flight time
Office of Aircraft Services Central Bill (administrative charges for OAS training, management, flight services, safety)	NPS	-	688	-	-	Flight time
Subtotal Program Assessments		*100*	*3,568*	*100*	*-*	
Bureau Administrative Costs						
Preparedness Indirect for Tribal Programs	BIA	2,245				Budget need
State Level Indirect (Admin support at the State, district, and field office level: procurement, HR, IT)	BLM	10,067	-	3,418	-	10% of State Base allocation
Regional Program Management Support Share: This includes regional assessments made to meet specific administrative support and Regional/Director priorities for that particular geographic region.	FWS	600	-	317	-	% of FTE
Subtotal Bureau Administrative Costs		*12,912*	*-*	*3,735*	*-*	
Total All Assessments and Reserves		23,422	3,614	7,399	-	14

BUDGET SCHEDULES

Budget Schedules

Program and Financing (Millions $) Identification code: 14-1125-0-1-302	2013 Actual	2014 Enacted	2015 Request
Obligations by program activity:			
0001 Preparedness (Readiness, Facilities, and Fire Science)	284	294	331
0004 Fire suppression operations	399	378	383
0006 Fuels Management	138	145	146
0007 Resilient Landscapes	0	0	30
0008 Burned area rehabilitation	12	16	18
0799 Total direct obligations	833	833	908
0801 Fire reimbursable	38	38	38
0900 Total new obligations	871	871	946
Budgetary Resources:			
1000 Unobligated balance brought forward, Oct 1	72	82	117
1011 Unobligated balance transfer from other accts [14-5035]	12	0	0
1011 Unobligated balance transfer from other accts [14-5033]	3	0	0
1011 Unobligated balance transfer from other accts [14-1612]	3	0	0
1011 Unobligated balance transfer from other accts [14-5020]	1	0	0
1011 Unobligated balance transfer from other accts [14-5143]	4	0	0
1011 Unobligated balance transfer from other accts [14-5496]	1	0	0
1011 Unobligated balance transfer from other accts [14-1039]	3	0	0
1021 Recoveries of prior year unpaid obligations	11	15	15
1050 Unobligated balance (total)	110	97	132
Budget authority:			
Appropriations, discretionary:			
1100 Appropriation	749	777	525
1100 Appropriation - Fire Suppression	0	0	269
1100 Appropriation - FLAME Suppression Cap Adj	0	0	240
1120 Appropriations transferred to other accts [12-1115]	-2	0	0
1120 Appropriations transferred to other accts [14-1039]	-16	0	0
1121 Appropriations transferred from other accts [14-1127]	92	92	0
1121 Appropriations transferred from other accts [14-1039]	4	0	0
1121 Appropriations transferred from other accts [12-1115]	6	0	0
1121 Appropriations transferred from other accts [14-5020]	1	0	0
1121 Appropriations transferred from other accts [14-5035]	1	0	0
1130 Appropriations permanently reduced	-42	0	0
1130 Appropriations permanently reduced	-1	0	0
1130 Appropriations permanently reduced	-7	0	0
1131 Unobligated balance of appropriations permanently reduced	0	-8	0
1160 Appropriation, discretionary (total)	785	861	1,034

Program and Financing (Millions $) Identification code: 14-1125-0-1-302	2013 Actual	2014 Enacted	2015 Request
Spending authority from offsetting collections, discretionary:			
1700 Collected	59	30	30
1701 Change in uncollected payments, Federal sources	-1	0	0
1750 Spending auth from offsetting collections, disc (total)	58	30	30
1900 Budget authority (total)	843	891	1,064
1930 Total budgetary resources available	953	988	1,196
Memorandum (non-add) entries:			
1941 Unexpired unobligated balance, end of year	82	117	250
Change in obligated balance:			
3000 Unpaid obligations, brought forward, Oct 1	298	250	315
3010 Obligations incurred, unexpired accounts	871	871	946
3020 Outlays (gross)	-908	-791	-1,018
3040 Recoveries of prior year unpaid obligations, unexpired	-11	-15	-15
3050 Unpaid obligations, end of year	250	315	228
3060 Uncollected pymts, Fed sources, brought forward, Oct 1	-13	-12	-12
3070 Change in uncollected pymts, Fed sources, unexpired	1	0	0
3090 Uncollected pymts, Fed sources, end of year	-12	-12	-12
Memorandum (non-add) entries:			
3100 Obligated balance, start of year	285	238	303
3200 Obligated balance, end of year	238	303	216
Budget authority and outlays, net:			
4000 Budget authority, gross	843	891	1,064
4010 Outlays from new discretionary authority	566	607	634
4011 Outlays from discretionary balances	342	184	384
4020 Outlays, gross (total)	908	791	1,018
Offsets against gross budget authority and outlays:			
4030 Federal sources	-11	-9	-9
4033 Non-Federal sources	-48	-21	-21
4040 Offsets against gross budget authority and outlays (total)	-59	-30	-30
4050 Change in uncollected pymts, Fed sources, unexpired	1	0	0
4070 Budget authority, net (discretionary)	785	861	1,034
4080 Outlays, net (discretionary)	849	761	988
4180 Budget authority, net (total)	785	861	1,034
4190 Outlays, net (total)	849	761	988

Program and Financing (Millions $) Identification code: 14-1125-0-1-302	BOC	2013 Actual	2014 Enacted	2015 Request
Direct obligations:				
Personnel compensation:				
Full-time permanent	11.1	3	3	3
Civilian personnel benefits	12.1	1	1	1
Other services from non-Federal sources	25.2	3	3	3
Other goods and services from Federal sources	25.3	2	2	2
Subtotal, obligations	99.0	9	9	9
Allocation Account - direct:				
Personnel compensation:				
Full-time permanent	11.1	183	235	268
Other than full-time permanent	11.3	21	15	20
Other personnel compensation	11.5	89	85	65
Special personal services payments	11.8	40	30	40
Total personnel compensation	11.9	333	365	393
Civilian personnel benefits	12.1	90	90	90
Travel and transportation of persons	21.0	20	20	20
Transportation of things	22.0	5	3	3
Rental payments to GSA	23.1	1	1	1
Rental payments to others	23.2	2	2	2
Communications, utilities, and miscellaneous charges	23.3	14	15	16
Advisory and assistance services	25.1	3	4	4
Other services from non-Federal sources	25.2	176	171	194
Other goods and services from Federal sources	25.3	89	82	90
Operation and maintenance of facilities	25.4	2	2	2
Medical care	25.6	1	1	1
Operation and maintenance of equipment	25.7	6	5	5
Subsistence and support of persons	25.8	0	1	1
Supplies and materials	26.0	38	30	40
Equipment	31.0	9	8	8
Land and structures	32.0	6	4	4
Grants, subsidies, and contributions	41.0	29	20	25
Subtotal, obligations	99.0	824	824	899

Program and Financing (Millions $) Identification code: 14-1125-0-1-302	BOC	2013 Actual	2014 Enacted	2015 Request
Allocation Account - reimbursable:				
Personnel compensation:				
Full-time permanent	11.1	5	5	5
Other than full-time permanent	11.3	1	1	1
Other personnel compensation	11.5	1	1	1
Total personnel compensation	11.9	7	7	7
Civilian personnel benefits	12.1	2	2	2
Travel and transportation of persons	21.0	1	1	1
Other services from non-Federal sources	25.2	18	19	19
Other goods and services from Federal sources	25.3	2	2	2
Supplies and materials	26.0	2	2	2
Equipment	31.0	0	1	1
Grants, subsidies, and contributions	41.0	6	4	4
Subtotal, obligations	99.0	38	38	38
Total new obligations	99.9	871	871	946

www.ingramcontent.com/pod-product-compliance
Lightning Source LLC
Chambersburg PA
CBHW081112290526
45795CB00006B/2093